I0767843

Get A Free Book At: xspurts.com/posts/free-book-offer

Table of Contents:

Never-Ending Fuzz: Understanding the Fascination with Beards

Beards have fascinated humanity for centuries, evoking a sense of rugged masculinity, wisdom, and individuality. From ancient civilizations to modern times, the appeal of facial hair has persisted, transcending cultural boundaries and societal norms. Understanding the psychology behind the fascination with beards reveals insights into human evolution, social perceptions, and individual identity.

One aspect of the allure of beards lies in their connection to masculinity and virility. Throughout history, beards have been associated with traits such as strength, dominance, and maturity, reflecting evolutionary signals of reproductive fitness and social status. In many cultures, the ability to grow a full beard is seen as a symbol of masculinity and maturity, signaling to others one's physical and social prowess. As a result, men may grow and maintain beards as a way to assert their masculinity and enhance their attractiveness to potential mates.

Moreover, beards can serve as expressions of individual identity and personal style. Just as clothing and hairstyles are used to convey personality and fashion preferences, beards offer a unique form of self-expression. Whether sporting a neatly trimmed beard, a rugged stubble, or a long, flowing mane, individuals can use facial hair to project their desired image to the world. Beards allow individuals to experiment with different styles, shapes, and lengths, allowing them to cultivate a look that aligns with their personality, values, and lifestyle.

Furthermore, the appeal of beards may stem from their association with wisdom, maturity, and authority. In many cultures, older individuals with full, gray beards are revered as wise elders and leaders, embodying qualities such as wisdom, experience, and knowledge. As such, the presence of a beard can confer an air of authority and respectability, commanding attention and admiration from others. For some individuals, growing a beard may be a way to assert their authority and establish their credibility in professional and social settings.

Additionally, the fascination with beards can be attributed to their role in shaping social perceptions and interactions. Research suggests that individuals with beards are often perceived as more masculine, mature, and dominant compared to their clean-shaven counterparts. Bearded individuals may be seen as more competent, trustworthy, and socially dominant, influencing how they are perceived and treated by others in various contexts. As a result, men may choose to grow beards as a way to enhance their social standing and assert their dominance in interpersonal interactions.

Moreover, the cultural and historical significance of beards contributes to their enduring appeal and fascination. Throughout history, beards have been associated with various religious, cultural, and social practices, playing important roles in rituals, ceremonies, and rites of passage. From the ancient Egyptians and Greeks to the Vikings and Samurai, beards have held symbolic meaning and cultural significance in diverse societies around the world. Today, the resurgence of interest in traditional grooming practices and retro fashion trends has fueled a renewed appreciation for beards, leading to their widespread popularity and acceptance in contemporary society.

In conclusion, the fascination with beards stems from a complex interplay of factors, including their association with masculinity, individual identity, wisdom, authority, and social perceptions. As symbols of masculinity, maturity, and individuality, beards offer a unique form of self-expression and personal style. Moreover, their cultural and historical significance contributes to their enduring appeal and fascination across different cultures and societies. Whether worn for personal expression, social status, or cultural tradition, beards continue to captivate the imagination and evoke a sense of admiration and intrigue in the minds of individuals around the world.

Evolutionary basis of beards

The evolutionary basis of beards provides fascinating insights into the role of facial hair in human evolution, social interactions, and sexual selection. While the exact reasons for the evolution of beards remain a subject of debate among scientists, several theories have been proposed to explain their emergence and persistence across human history.

One prominent theory suggests that beards evolved as a secondary sexual characteristic, signaling reproductive fitness and mate quality. In many species, males develop exaggerated traits such as colorful plumage or elaborate antlers to attract mates and compete for reproductive opportunities. Similarly, the ability to grow a full beard may have served as a signal of masculinity, dominance, and genetic quality in ancestral human populations. A thick, lustrous beard could have signaled to potential mates that an individual was healthy, virile, and capable of providing for offspring, making bearded men more attractive and desirable as mates.

Moreover, the presence of facial hair may have provided an evolutionary advantage by offering protection against environmental hazards and physical harm. In ancestral environments, where humans lived as hunter-gatherers exposed to the elements and natural predators, a thick beard could have served as a form of natural insulation, protecting the face and neck from cold temperatures, windburn, and sun exposure. Additionally, facial hair may have helped cushion blows to the face during interpersonal conflicts or hunting activities, reducing the risk of injury and increasing survival chances.

Furthermore, beards may have played a role in social signaling and group cohesion among early human societies. In many cultures, facial hair is associated with maturity, wisdom, and social status, with older individuals often sporting full, gray beards as a sign of respectability and authority. In tribal societies, beards may have served as markers of group affiliation and identity, distinguishing members of different clans or social hierarchies. The presence of a beard could have signaled an individual's status within the community, influencing social interactions, alliances, and leadership dynamics.

Additionally, the evolution of beards may be linked to sexual selection and mate choice preferences. Research suggests that mate preferences vary across cultures and contexts, with some individuals expressing a preference for bearded partners while others prefer clean-shaven faces. In societies where beards are valued as symbols of masculinity and attractiveness, individuals with facial hair may have a competitive advantage in attracting mates and securing reproductive opportunities. Conversely, in cultures where smooth, youthful faces are preferred, individuals may invest in grooming practices such as shaving to enhance their perceived attractiveness and social desirability.

Overall, the evolutionary basis of beards highlights the complex interplay between biological, cultural, and social factors in shaping human behavior and appearance. While the exact reasons for the evolution of facial hair remain speculative, it is clear that beards have played important roles in human evolution, social interactions, and mate choice throughout history. Whether as signals of reproductive fitness, protective adaptations, or markers of social status, beards continue to hold significance in modern society, reflecting our deep-rooted evolutionary heritage and cultural diversity.

Beards in human history

Throughout human history, beards have played a prominent and diverse role in shaping cultural norms, religious beliefs, social status, and individual identity. From ancient civilizations to modern times, facial hair has been both celebrated and stigmatized, reflecting the ever-evolving attitudes and perceptions surrounding masculinity, beauty, and self-expression.

In ancient civilizations such as Egypt, Mesopotamia, and Greece, beards held symbolic significance and cultural importance. Among the ancient Egyptians, beards were associated with divinity and wisdom, with pharaohs and gods often depicted with full, flowing beards to convey their authority and divine status. Similarly, in ancient Mesopotamia, beards were seen as a symbol of virility and masculinity, and men would often groom and adorn their facial hair as a mark of social status and power. In ancient Greece, beards were regarded as a sign of wisdom and maturity, and philosophers such as Socrates and Plato were known for their long, bushy beards, which were seen as symbols of intellectual prowess and philosophical insight.

During the Middle Ages in Europe, beards continued to be associated with masculinity, honor, and nobility. Knights and noblemen would often wear elaborate beards as a sign of their status and chivalry, while peasants and commoners were typically clean-shaven. Beards were also closely linked to religious beliefs and practices, with many religious figures and ascetics growing long, unkempt beards as a sign of piety and devotion. In Christianity, for example, beards were often associated with prophets, saints, and religious leaders, and the shaving of one's beard was sometimes considered a sign of mourning or penance.

However, attitudes towards beards began to shift during the Renaissance and the Enlightenment, as Western societies increasingly embraced ideals of rationality, cleanliness, and refinement. In the 17th and 18th centuries, clean-shaven faces became fashionable among European elites, reflecting a desire for sophistication and modernity. Beards were often associated with barbarism, backwardness, and uncleanliness, and men were encouraged to shave their facial hair as a mark of social progress and civility.

Nevertheless, the 19th and 20th centuries witnessed a resurgence of interest in facial hair, as beards once again became symbols of masculinity, rebellion, and counterculture. During the Victorian era, beards experienced a revival in popularity among European and American men, with prominent figures such as Charles Darwin, Abraham Lincoln, and Karl Marx sporting distinctive facial hair styles. Similarly, in the 1960s and 1970s, the hippie movement embraced facial hair as a form of anti-establishment protest, with long, unkempt beards becoming a symbol of youthful rebellion and nonconformity.

In recent decades, beards have experienced a resurgence in popularity, as changing cultural attitudes and grooming trends have led to a renewed interest in facial hair among men of all ages. Today, beards are celebrated as expressions of individuality, style, and self-confidence, with a wide range of grooming products and techniques available to help men achieve their desired look. Whether worn as a symbol of masculinity, wisdom, or personal style, beards continue to hold cultural significance and social meaning in the modern world, reflecting our ever-evolving understanding of beauty, identity, and self-expression.

Cultural influence on beards

Cultural influences play a significant role in shaping attitudes towards beards, determining their meaning, acceptance, and prevalence across different societies and historical periods. From ancient civilizations to modern-day cultures, the perception of facial hair varies widely, reflecting a complex interplay of religious, social, and historical factors.

In many cultures, beards have been revered as symbols of masculinity, wisdom, and social status. In ancient Egypt, for example, pharaohs and noblemen adorned themselves with elaborate beards to convey their authority and divine status. Similarly, in ancient Greece, beards were associated with virility, maturity, and intellectual prowess, with philosophers and scholars often depicted with full, bushy beards as a sign of wisdom and insight.

Conversely, in some cultures, facial hair has been viewed with suspicion or disdain, associated with notions of barbarism, savagery, or religious impurity. In ancient Rome, for instance, beards were often seen as a mark of uncivilized behavior, and Roman men were encouraged to maintain clean-shaven faces as a sign of cultural refinement and sophistication. Similarly, in medieval Europe, beards were sometimes associated with heresy or witchcraft, and men accused of practicing forbidden beliefs or behaviors were often depicted with long, unkempt beards as a sign of their moral degeneracy.

Religious beliefs and traditions have also played a significant role in shaping cultural attitudes towards beards. In many religious traditions, facial hair holds symbolic significance and carries religious mandates or prohibitions. In Islam, for example, growing a beard is considered a Sunnah, or religious practice, based on the teachings of the Prophet Muhammad. Many devout Muslim men grow beards as an expression of their faith and adherence to Islamic traditions. Similarly, in Sikhism, maintaining uncut hair, including facial hair, is one of the Five Ks, or articles of faith, representing a commitment to the Sikh way of life and identity.

Moreover, cultural norms and grooming practices vary widely across different regions and societies, influencing the prevalence and acceptance of facial hair. In some cultures, such as those in the Middle East or South Asia, full beards are commonly worn by men as a sign of masculinity, virility, and cultural identity. In other cultures, such as those in East Asia or parts of Europe, clean-shaven faces are more prevalent and are often associated with professionalism, cleanliness, and modernity.

The influence of popular culture and media has also played a significant role in shaping attitudes towards beards in modern society. In recent years, beards have experienced a resurgence in popularity, with celebrities, athletes, and influencers often sporting fashionable facial hair styles. From the rugged stubble of Hollywood heartthrobs to the meticulously groomed beards of hipster trendsetters, facial hair has become a prominent feature of contemporary fashion and pop culture, influencing grooming trends and beauty standards around the world.

In conclusion, cultural influences have played a pivotal role in shaping attitudes towards beards throughout history and across different societies. Whether revered as symbols of masculinity and wisdom or viewed with suspicion as signs of barbarism or religious impurity, facial hair holds diverse meanings and significance across cultures, reflecting the rich tapestry of human beliefs, traditions, and social norms.

Psychology of Beards: Deeper than Skin

The psychology of beards delves into the intricate relationship between facial hair and human behavior, perception, and identity. Beyond mere physical appearance, beards can influence individuals' self-perception, social interactions, and even professional success, reflecting deep-rooted psychological processes and societal norms.

One key aspect of the psychology of beards is the role they play in shaping perceptions of masculinity. Across cultures and historical periods, facial hair has often been associated with masculinity, strength, and virility. The presence or absence of a beard can significantly impact how individuals are perceived by others and how they perceive themselves. Studies have shown that men with beards are often perceived as more mature, dominant, and socially mature than their clean-shaven counterparts. This perception of bearded individuals as more masculine and dominant can influence various aspects of social interaction, including mate selection, competition, and leadership roles.

Moreover, facial hair can also serve as a form of self-expression and identity construction. For many individuals, growing a beard is a deliberate choice that reflects their personal values, beliefs, and identity. Whether embracing a rugged, unkempt look or maintaining a meticulously groomed beard, individuals often use facial hair as a means of expressing their individuality and asserting their identity. In this way, beards can serve as a powerful tool for self-expression and self-assertion, allowing individuals to project a certain image or persona to the world.

Furthermore, the psychology of beards also encompasses the impact of facial hair on social perception and professional success. While beards are often associated with masculinity and maturity, they can also evoke different impressions depending on cultural and social contexts. In some professional settings, for example, beards may be perceived as unprofessional or unkempt, leading individuals to shave or groom their facial hair to conform to workplace norms. Conversely, in other contexts, such as creative industries or countercultural movements, beards may be embraced as a symbol of authenticity, creativity, and nonconformity.

Additionally, the psychology of beards extends to the realm of evolutionary psychology, exploring the adaptive significance of facial hair in human evolution. Some researchers argue that facial hair may have evolved as a form of sexual signaling, allowing men to display their physical fitness and reproductive potential to potential mates. Others suggest that beards may have served as a form of protection against physical injury or aggression, providing a cushioning layer of hair to absorb impacts and protect sensitive facial features.

Overall, the psychology of beards is a multifaceted and complex field of study that encompasses a wide range of psychological, social, and evolutionary processes. From shaping perceptions of masculinity and identity to influencing social interactions and professional success, facial hair holds significant psychological and cultural significance. By exploring the psychology of beards, researchers can gain valuable insights into human behavior, identity construction, and social dynamics, shedding light on the deeper psychological processes underlying this seemingly mundane aspect of human appearance.

The theory of masculinity and beards

The theory of masculinity and beards explores the intricate relationship between facial hair and the construction of masculine identity. Throughout history and across cultures, beards have been closely associated with masculinity, symbolizing strength, virility, and maturity. The theory delves into the psychological and sociocultural factors that underlie this association, shedding light on how beards shape perceptions of masculinity and influence men's sense of self.

One key aspect of the theory of masculinity and beards is the idea that facial hair serves as a visible marker of male secondary sexual characteristics. From an evolutionary perspective, beards may have evolved as a sexually dimorphic trait, signaling reproductive fitness and mate quality to potential partners. According to this theory, the ability to grow a full, thick beard may indicate high levels of testosterone and genetic fitness, making bearded individuals more attractive to potential mates. As a result, men may grow beards as a means of enhancing their sexual attractiveness and signaling their masculinity to others.

Moreover, the theory of masculinity and beards explores the cultural significance of facial hair as a symbol of social status and power. Across many cultures and historical periods, beards have been associated with authority, wisdom, and leadership. In ancient civilizations such as Egypt and Greece, beards were often worn by rulers, noblemen, and philosophers as a sign of their elevated social status and intellectual prowess. Even today, beards are sometimes perceived as a symbol of masculinity and authority, with men in positions of power often sporting full, well-groomed beards to project a sense of confidence and authority.

Furthermore, the theory of masculinity and beards considers the role of social norms and expectations in shaping men's grooming behaviors. In many cultures, facial hair is seen as a natural expression of masculinity, and men may feel pressure to conform to societal expectations by growing or maintaining beards. Conversely, in cultures where clean-shaven faces are the norm, men who choose to grow beards may face stigma or discrimination for deviating from established grooming norms. This dynamic illustrates how societal attitudes towards facial hair can influence men's grooming choices and perceptions of masculinity.

Additionally, the theory of masculinity and beards examines the intersectionality of gender, race, and class in shaping perceptions of facial hair. While beards are often associated with white masculinity in Western cultures, they may carry different connotations for men of color. For example, Black men may face racial profiling or discrimination based on their facial hair, with beards being perceived as a sign of criminality or threat. Similarly, men from lower socioeconomic backgrounds may be more likely to wear beards as a means of asserting their masculinity and social status in the absence of other forms of cultural capital.

In conclusion, the theory of masculinity and beards offers valuable insights into the complex interplay of biological, cultural, and social factors that shape perceptions of masculinity and influence men's grooming behaviors. By understanding the psychological and sociocultural significance of facial hair, researchers can gain a deeper understanding of how beards contribute to the construction of masculine identity and influence men's sense of self in diverse cultural contexts.

Beards as a sign of maturity

Beards have long been regarded as a sign of maturity across various cultures and historical periods. This perception stems from a combination of biological, social, and psychological factors that contribute to the association between facial hair and maturity.

Biologically, the ability to grow a beard typically occurs during puberty, a period marked by physical and hormonal changes that signal the transition from childhood to adulthood. As such, the presence of facial hair is often seen as a visible marker of sexual maturation and physical development. In many cultures, the onset of beard growth is celebrated as a rite of passage, symbolizing the emergence of masculinity and the assumption of adult responsibilities.

Moreover, the association between beards and maturity is reinforced by societal norms and expectations surrounding grooming and appearance. In many cultures, clean-shaven faces are associated with youthfulness and innocence, while beards are seen as a symbol of maturity, wisdom, and experience. This perception is reflected in popular culture, where bearded characters are often portrayed as wise mentors or authoritative figures, further reinforcing the idea that facial hair is synonymous with maturity.

Psychologically, the presence of a beard can also influence how individuals perceive themselves and how they are perceived by others. Research suggests that men with beards are often perceived as older, more mature, and more dominant than their clean-shaven counterparts. This perception can have a profound impact on individuals' self-image and self-esteem, influencing their behavior and interactions with others.

Furthermore, the association between beards and maturity extends beyond mere physical appearance to encompass broader aspects of social and emotional development. Men with beards may be perceived as more mature and capable of handling responsibilities, leading to greater respect and admiration from others. This can be particularly relevant in professional settings, where individuals with beards may be seen as more competent and trustworthy than those without.

In addition to cultural and social factors, the association between beards and maturity may also be influenced by individual differences in personality and self-perception. For some men, growing a beard may be a conscious decision to assert their maturity and masculinity, while for others, it may simply be a matter of personal preference or convenience. Regardless of the reasons behind it, the presence of facial hair often carries with it connotations of maturity, wisdom, and authority.

However, it is important to note that the perception of beards as a sign of maturity is not universal and may vary depending on cultural and social context. In some cultures, for example, beards may be associated with religious or spiritual significance rather than maturity per se. Similarly, attitudes towards facial hair may change over time, with different generations and subcultures interpreting its meaning in distinct ways.

In conclusion, the association between beards and maturity is a complex and multifaceted phenomenon that reflects a combination of biological, social, and psychological factors. Whether seen as a symbol of physical maturation, social status, or personal identity, facial hair holds significant cultural significance as a marker of maturity and adulthood. Understanding the psychology of beards and their role in shaping perceptions of maturity can provide valuable insights into the ways in which appearance influences social interactions, self-image, and identity formation.

The rebellion icon: Beards and counter-culture

Throughout history, beards have often been associated with rebellion and counterculture, serving as a visual symbol of defiance against mainstream norms and values. From the beatniks of the 1950s to the hippies of the 1960s and the punks of the 1970s, beards have been embraced by various subcultures as a means of expressing dissent and challenging societal conventions.

One reason for the association between beards and counter-culture is the historical context in which facial hair has been viewed. In Western societies, particularly in the 20th century, clean-shaven faces were often considered the norm, associated with professionalism, conformity, and respectability. In contrast, beards were seen as a rejection of these mainstream ideals, signaling a desire to break free from societal constraints and embrace alternative lifestyles.

Moreover, the act of growing a beard can be seen as a form of personal expression and self-assertion. By choosing to cultivate facial hair, individuals can assert their autonomy and reject societal expectations regarding grooming and appearance. In this sense, beards become a means of asserting individuality and asserting one's identity in the face of societal pressure to conform.

Additionally, beards have been adopted by various countercultural movements as a symbol of solidarity and resistance. During the 1960s, for example, the hippie movement embraced long, unkempt beards as a rejection of mainstream consumerism and materialism, instead espousing values of peace, love, and communal living. Similarly, in the punk subculture of the 1970s, beards became associated with anti-establishment attitudes and a rejection of traditional authority figures.

Furthermore, the symbolism of beards in counter-culture extends beyond mere physical appearance to encompass broader ideas of authenticity and non-conformity. By eschewing mainstream grooming norms and embracing facial hair, individuals can signal their rejection of societal norms and embrace alternative ways of living and thinking. In this way, beards become a form of cultural resistance, challenging dominant narratives and offering alternative visions of identity and belonging.

However, it is important to recognize that the association between beards and counter-culture is not limited to any particular time period or social movement. Throughout history, beards have been embraced by individuals seeking to challenge existing power structures and assert their autonomy and individuality. Whether in the form of the bohemian artists of the 19th century or the hipsters of the 21st century, beards continue to serve as a potent symbol of rebellion and non-conformity.

In conclusion, the association between beards and counter-culture reflects a complex interplay of historical, cultural, and social factors. From the beat generation to the present day, facial hair has served as a powerful symbol of rebellion and dissent, signaling a rejection of mainstream norms and values. By embracing beards, individuals can assert their autonomy and assert their identity in the face of societal pressure to conform. As such, beards continue to hold a unique place in the cultural landscape, serving as an enduring symbol of resistance and non-conformity.

Beard Personality: Prediction & Reality

The idea that a person's beard reflects their personality has long been a subject of fascination and speculation. While some may dismiss it as a mere stereotype, there is evidence to suggest that there may indeed be a link between facial hair and certain personality traits, although it is important to approach such claims with caution.

One of the most common stereotypes associated with beards is that they convey a sense of masculinity and ruggedness. Indeed, throughout history, men with full, well-groomed beards have often been seen as strong, assertive, and confident. This perception may be rooted in evolutionary psychology, which suggests that facial hair signals sexual maturity and dominance, traits traditionally associated with masculinity.

Furthermore, the decision to grow and maintain a beard can be seen as a reflection of individual values and attitudes. Some men may choose to grow a beard as a way of expressing their independence and non-conformity, while others may see it as a symbol of tradition and heritage. As such, the presence or absence of facial hair can offer insight into a person's self-image and sense of identity.

In addition to conveying masculinity, facial hair may also be associated with other personality traits, such as creativity and eccentricity. This idea is supported by research suggesting that people with beards are often perceived as more artistic, unconventional, and free-spirited than their clean-shaven counterparts. This perception may be influenced by cultural stereotypes that portray bearded individuals as bohemian artists or eccentric intellectuals.

However, it is important to recognize that the link between facial hair and personality is not straightforward and may vary depending on individual differences and cultural context. While some may see beards as a sign of strength and confidence, others may perceive them as a sign of unkemptness or laziness. Similarly, cultural attitudes towards facial hair can vary widely, with some societies valuing beards as a symbol of wisdom and maturity, while others see them as a sign of backwardness or primitiveness.

Moreover, the relationship between facial hair and personality is not limited to men. In recent years, growing numbers of women have embraced facial hair as a form of self-expression and empowerment. Whether in the form of bold statement beards or subtle facial hair grooming, women with facial hair challenge traditional gender norms and offer alternative visions of beauty and femininity.

In conclusion, while the idea that a person's beard reflects their personality may be based in part on cultural stereotypes and perceptions, there is evidence to suggest that facial hair can offer insight into individual values, attitudes, and self-image. Whether seen as a symbol of masculinity, creativity, or non-conformity, beards continue to hold a unique place in the cultural landscape, shaping perceptions of identity and self-expression. As such, the psychology of beards remains a fascinating and complex topic worthy of further exploration and study.

Beards and first impressions

Beards have a significant impact on first impressions, shaping how individuals are perceived by others in social and professional settings. Research suggests that facial hair plays a crucial role in forming initial judgments and impressions, influencing perceptions of attractiveness, trustworthiness, and competence.

One of the key factors that influence first impressions of individuals with beards is attractiveness. Studies have shown that facial hair can enhance perceptions of attractiveness in men, with full, well-groomed beards often seen as a sign of masculinity and virility. However, the appeal of beards varies depending on individual preferences and cultural norms. While some may find beards attractive and appealing, others may see them as unattractive or unkempt.

Moreover, facial hair can also influence perceptions of trustworthiness and competence. Research suggests that men with beards are often perceived as more mature, experienced, and authoritative than their clean-shaven counterparts. This perception may be rooted in cultural stereotypes that associate facial hair with wisdom and maturity. However, perceptions of trustworthiness and competence can also be influenced by factors such as grooming, style, and facial symmetry.

Furthermore, the impact of facial hair on first impressions extends beyond individual perceptions to include societal norms and expectations. In many cultures, facial hair is seen as a symbol of masculinity and maturity, with men often expected to grow and maintain beards as a sign of social status and respectability. As such, individuals with beards may be viewed more favorably in certain social and professional contexts, particularly those that value traditional gender roles and norms.

However, it is important to recognize that the perception of facial hair can vary depending on individual differences and cultural context. While some may see beards as a sign of maturity and authority, others may perceive them as a sign of unprofessionalism or non-conformity. Moreover, perceptions of facial hair may also be influenced by factors such as race, ethnicity, and social class, with certain groups facing stigma or discrimination based on their appearance.

In conclusion, facial hair plays a significant role in shaping first impressions, influencing perceptions of attractiveness, trustworthiness, and competence. Whether seen as a sign of masculinity and maturity or as a symbol of non-conformity and rebellion, beards have a powerful impact on how individuals are perceived by others in social and professional settings. As such, the psychology of beards continues to be a fascinating and complex topic worthy of further exploration and study.

Research on beard personalities

Research on beard personalities delves into the intriguing relationship between facial hair and various personality traits, shedding light on the psychological dynamics associated with different beard styles and grooming practices. Studies in this field explore how beards can influence perceptions of masculinity, attractiveness, and social status, as well as how they can shape self-image and identity.

One area of research focuses on the perceived masculinity of different beard styles. Studies have found that full, thick beards are often associated with traits such as dominance, assertiveness, and strength, reflecting cultural ideals of traditional masculinity. On the other hand, shorter, neater beard styles may be seen as more refined and sophisticated, conveying a sense of maturity and professionalism. These findings suggest that the choice of beard style can reflect and reinforce perceptions of masculinity, influencing how individuals are perceived by others in social and professional contexts.

Furthermore, research has also examined the impact of facial hair on perceptions of attractiveness. Studies consistently show that facial hair can enhance perceptions of attractiveness in men, particularly when it is well-groomed and maintained. However, the appeal of facial hair may vary depending on individual preferences and cultural norms. While some may find beards attractive and appealing, others may prefer a clean-shaven look. Understanding the factors that influence perceptions of attractiveness can provide valuable insights into the role of facial hair in interpersonal relationships and mate selection.

Moreover, research on beard personalities has explored the social and psychological factors that influence the decision to grow and maintain a beard. Studies have found that men with beards often report higher levels of self-confidence and self-esteem, as well as a greater sense of identity and self-expression. Additionally, facial hair grooming practices may be influenced by cultural and societal norms, as well as individual values and beliefs. For example, some men may choose to grow a beard as a way of asserting their masculinity and independence, while others may see it as a form of self-expression and personal style.

Another area of research examines the relationship between facial hair and social status. Studies have found that men with beards are often perceived as more mature, experienced, and authoritative than their clean-shaven counterparts, reflecting cultural stereotypes that associate facial hair with wisdom and respectability. However, perceptions of social status may also be influenced by factors such as grooming, style, and facial symmetry. Understanding how facial hair can influence perceptions of social status can provide valuable insights into the role of appearance in social interactions and professional settings.

In conclusion, research on beard personalities offers valuable insights into the psychological dynamics associated with facial hair. By exploring how different beard styles and grooming practices can influence perceptions of masculinity, attractiveness, and social status, researchers can gain a better understanding of the role of facial hair in shaping self-image, identity, and interpersonal relationships. As such, the psychology of beards continues to be a fascinating and evolving field of study.

The Workplace Beard: Navigating Corporate Culture

Navigating corporate culture with a beard can present both opportunities and challenges for individuals in the workplace. The decision to grow and maintain facial hair in professional settings can be influenced by a variety of factors, including personal preferences, cultural norms, and company policies.

One of the key considerations for individuals with beards in the workplace is how their facial hair may be perceived by colleagues, clients, and superiors. While facial hair styles have become more widely accepted in many industries, there may still be lingering stereotypes or biases associated with certain beard styles. For example, full, unkempt beards may be seen as unprofessional or sloppy, while shorter, well-groomed beards may be viewed more favorably.

Moreover, the perception of facial hair in the workplace can vary depending on individual preferences and cultural norms. In some industries, such as creative fields or tech startups, facial hair may be seen as a sign of creativity, individuality, and authenticity. However, in more conservative industries, such as finance or law, facial hair may be viewed with skepticism or disapproval, particularly in client-facing roles.

Furthermore, company policies and dress codes may also impact how facial hair is perceived and regulated in the workplace. Some companies may have strict grooming policies that require employees to maintain a clean-shaven appearance, while others may have more relaxed policies that allow for beards and other facial hair styles. Understanding and adhering to company policies is essential for individuals with beards who want to navigate corporate culture successfully.

Despite the challenges, having a beard in the workplace can also confer certain advantages. Research suggests that facial hair can enhance perceptions of maturity, authority, and competence, which may be advantageous in leadership roles or when negotiating with clients and stakeholders. Additionally, facial hair can also serve as a form of self-expression and personal style, allowing individuals to project their identity and values in the workplace.

However, it is important for individuals with beards to be mindful of their grooming habits and appearance in the workplace. Maintaining a well-groomed and professional-looking beard can help mitigate any negative perceptions and ensure that facial hair is seen as a positive attribute rather than a distraction or liability.

In conclusion, navigating corporate culture with a beard requires individuals to consider a variety of factors, including personal preferences, cultural norms, company policies, and professional expectations. While facial hair can confer certain advantages in the workplace, it is important for individuals to be mindful of how their appearance may be perceived by others and to take steps to ensure that their grooming habits align with professional standards. By understanding and navigating the dynamics of workplace culture, individuals with beards can successfully integrate their personal style and identity into professional settings.

Perception of beards at work

The perception of beards in the workplace is a multifaceted issue influenced by a variety of factors, including cultural norms, individual preferences, and professional expectations. While facial hair styles have become increasingly accepted in many workplaces, there are still diverse perceptions of beards that can impact how individuals are perceived and treated in professional settings.

One aspect of the perception of beards at work is how facial hair is associated with certain personality traits and characteristics. Research suggests that individuals with beards may be perceived as more mature, experienced, and authoritative than their clean-shaven counterparts. Beards are often associated with traits such as wisdom, strength, and masculinity, reflecting cultural stereotypes and ideals of traditional masculinity.

Moreover, the perception of beards in the workplace can also be influenced by cultural and societal norms. In some cultures, facial hair is seen as a symbol of masculinity, virility, and wisdom, while in others, it may be associated with rebellion or nonconformity. Understanding the cultural context in which facial hair is perceived can provide valuable insights into how individuals with beards are viewed in different workplace environments.

Additionally, the perception of beards at work can vary depending on individual preferences and personal grooming habits. While some may view beards as a positive attribute that adds character and personality to one's appearance, others may see them as unprofessional or unkempt. Factors such as grooming, style, and maintenance can all impact how facial hair is perceived by colleagues, clients, and superiors in the workplace.

Furthermore, the perception of beards in the workplace may also be influenced by professional expectations and industry norms. In certain industries, such as creative fields or tech startups, facial hair may be more widely accepted and even celebrated as a sign of creativity and individuality. However, in more conservative industries, such as finance or law, facial hair may be viewed with skepticism or disapproval, particularly in client-facing roles.

Despite these diverse perceptions, research suggests that the overall perception of beards in the workplace has become more positive in recent years. With the rise of the "hipster" culture and the growing acceptance of diverse grooming styles, facial hair is increasingly seen as a form of self-expression and personal style rather than a reflection of professionalism or competence.

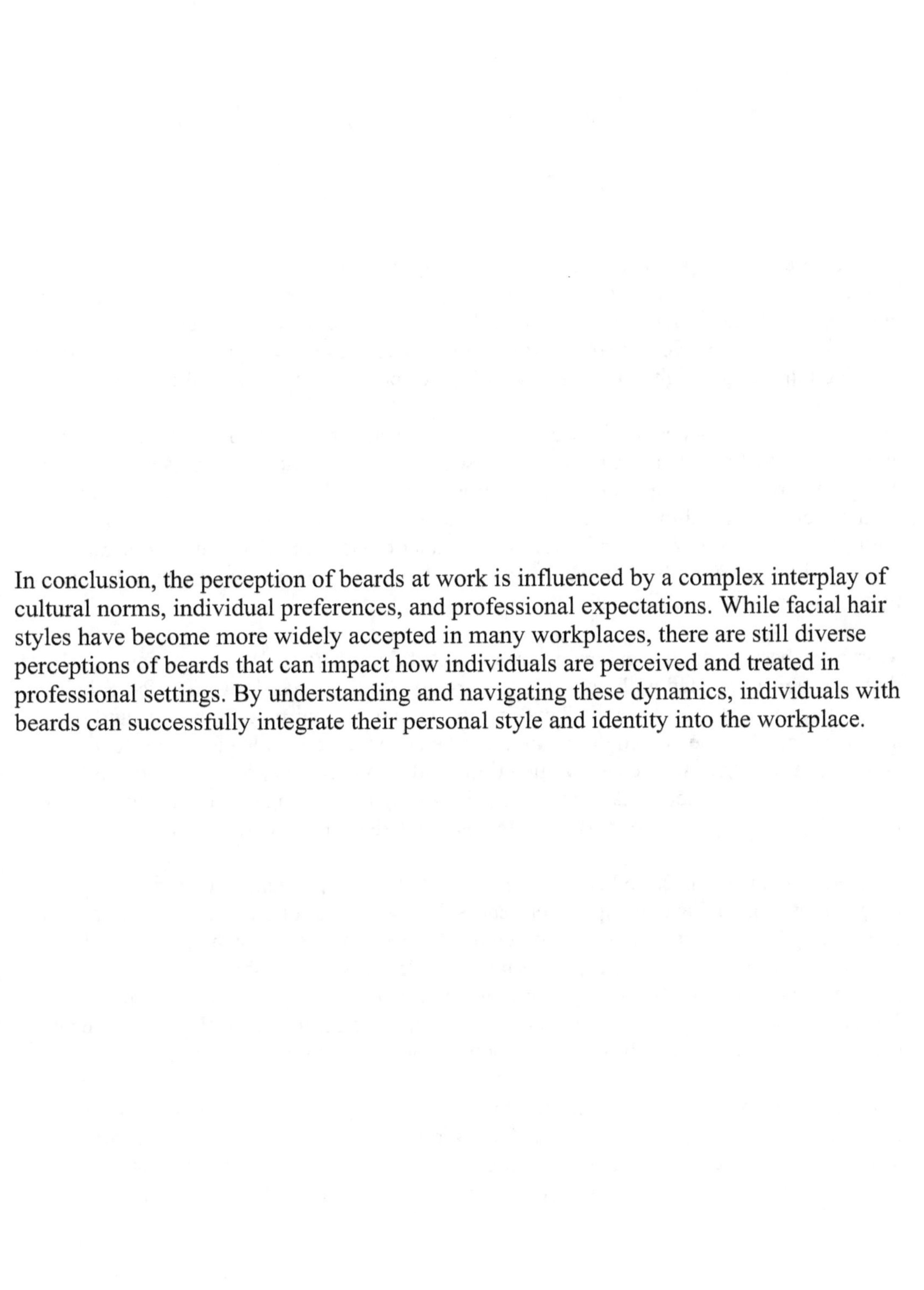

In conclusion, the perception of beards at work is influenced by a complex interplay of cultural norms, individual preferences, and professional expectations. While facial hair styles have become more widely accepted in many workplaces, there are still diverse perceptions of beards that can impact how individuals are perceived and treated in professional settings. By understanding and navigating these dynamics, individuals with beards can successfully integrate their personal style and identity into the workplace.

Beards and leadership: A surprising connection

In recent years, there has been a growing interest in exploring the relationship between beards and leadership, uncovering a surprising connection that challenges conventional perceptions. While facial hair has historically been associated with masculinity and authority, the link between beards and leadership qualities goes beyond mere stereotypes, offering intriguing insights into the psychology of beards in professional contexts.

One aspect of the connection between beards and leadership is the perception of maturity and wisdom that facial hair can convey. Research suggests that individuals with beards are often perceived as older and more experienced, traits that are commonly associated with effective leadership. In many cultures, facial hair has long been seen as a symbol of maturity and wisdom, reflecting traditional ideals of masculinity and authority. As a result, individuals with beards may be perceived as more capable and trustworthy leaders by their peers and subordinates.

Moreover, beards can also enhance perceptions of dominance and assertiveness, qualities that are often associated with effective leadership. Studies have shown that facial hair can accentuate the features of the face, making individuals appear more dominant and commanding. This perceived dominance can be advantageous in leadership roles, where assertiveness and confidence are valued traits. Additionally, the presence of facial hair may also signal to others that an individual is willing to challenge social norms and assert their independence, qualities that are often associated with successful leaders.

Furthermore, the connection between beards and leadership extends beyond mere perceptions to actual leadership effectiveness. Research has found that individuals with beards may be perceived as more competent and capable leaders by their peers and subordinates. This perception can have tangible effects on leadership outcomes, influencing decisions related to promotions, job assignments, and team dynamics. Moreover, individuals with beards may also benefit from enhanced self-confidence and self-perception, which can further contribute to their effectiveness as leaders.

However, it is important to recognize that the relationship between beards and leadership is not without its complexities and nuances. While facial hair may confer certain advantages in leadership roles, it is not a guarantee of leadership effectiveness. Leadership is a multifaceted construct that encompasses a wide range of skills and qualities, and the presence or absence of facial hair is just one of many factors that can influence perceptions of leadership.

Additionally, the perception of beards in leadership may also vary depending on cultural and organizational norms. In some industries and workplaces, facial hair may be viewed with skepticism or disapproval, particularly in client-facing roles or more conservative environments. As such, individuals with beards may need to navigate these cultural and organizational dynamics carefully to ensure that their facial hair does not hinder their leadership potential.

In conclusion, the connection between beards and leadership is a fascinating area of study that challenges conventional perceptions and offers new insights into the psychology of beards in professional contexts. While facial hair has long been associated with masculinity and authority, research suggests that it can also enhance perceptions of maturity, dominance, and leadership effectiveness. By understanding and leveraging these dynamics, individuals with beards can enhance their leadership potential and effectiveness in the workplace.

Beard and Attraction: The Romance of the Unshaven

The allure of facial hair has long captured the imagination, sparking debates and discussions about its impact on attractiveness and desirability. Beards, in particular, have emerged as a symbol of masculinity and rugged charm, captivating individuals with their rugged appeal. The psychology of beards in relation to attraction delves into the complex interplay of biology, culture, and personal preferences that shape our perceptions of facial hair and its romantic appeal.

From an evolutionary perspective, beards are often associated with traits such as strength, virility, and dominance, which are considered desirable qualities in a potential mate. Throughout history, facial hair has been linked to masculinity and sexual prowess, with bearded individuals often regarded as more attractive and sexually appealing. This evolutionary perspective suggests that our attraction to beards may be rooted in deep-seated biological instincts that drive us to seek out partners who possess traits associated with reproductive success.

However, the appeal of beards extends beyond mere biological factors to encompass cultural and social influences that shape our perceptions of attractiveness. In many societies, beards have been celebrated as a symbol of masculinity and maturity, imbued with connotations of strength, wisdom, and authority. As such, individuals with beards may be perceived as more confident, assertive, and attractive by others, reflecting societal norms and ideals of beauty.

Moreover, the psychology of attraction to beards is also influenced by individual preferences and personal experiences. Research suggests that people's perceptions of facial hair can vary widely based on factors such as upbringing, cultural background, and past experiences. For some individuals, beards may evoke feelings of admiration, desire, and fascination, while for others, they may be seen as unkempt, unappealing, or even intimidating. These individual differences highlight the subjective nature of attraction and the diversity of preferences when it comes to facial hair.

Furthermore, the appeal of beards in romantic contexts may also be influenced by socio-cultural factors such as media representation and celebrity culture. In recent years, beards have experienced a resurgence in popularity, with many celebrities and public figures sporting facial hair as a fashion statement. This increased visibility of beards in the media has helped to normalize and even glamorize facial hair, shaping perceptions of attractiveness and desirability among the general population.

In addition to cultural influences, the psychology of attraction to beards is also shaped by psychological theories such as the "mere-exposure effect" and the "halo effect." The mere-exposure effect suggests that repeated exposure to a stimulus, such as facial hair, can lead to increased familiarity and liking over time. Similarly, the halo effect posits that positive attributes associated with facial hair, such as masculinity and confidence, can influence perceptions of other traits, such as attractiveness and charm.

Overall, the psychology of attraction to beards is a multifaceted phenomenon that reflects a complex interplay of biological, cultural, and psychological factors. While evolutionary instincts may play a role in our preference for facial hair, cultural norms, individual preferences, and social influences also shape our perceptions of attractiveness and desirability. As such, the allure of beards in romantic contexts is a fascinating area of study that offers valuable insights into the complexities of human attraction and the role of facial hair in shaping romantic relationships.

Beards and physical attraction: A woman's perspective

The allure of beards has captivated individuals for centuries, sparking debates and discussions about their impact on physical attractiveness. From a woman's perspective, the psychology of beards in relation to physical attraction delves into the complex interplay of biology, culture, and personal preferences that shape perceptions of facial hair and its appeal.

Evolutionary theories suggest that facial hair, including beards, may be viewed as a sign of masculinity and reproductive fitness, traits that are inherently attractive to women seeking potential mates. Throughout history, beards have been associated with traits such as strength, virility, and dominance, qualities that are often considered desirable in a partner. From an evolutionary perspective, women may be drawn to bearded individuals as they perceive them to possess genetic qualities that could enhance the survival and reproductive success of their offspring.

Cultural influences also play a significant role in shaping women's perceptions of beards and their attractiveness. In many societies, beards have been celebrated as a symbol of masculinity and maturity, imbued with connotations of wisdom, strength, and authority. As such, women may find bearded men attractive due to societal norms and ideals of beauty that equate facial hair with desirable masculine traits.

Moreover, individual preferences and personal experiences also play a crucial role in shaping women's attraction to beards. Research suggests that women's perceptions of facial hair can vary widely based on factors such as upbringing, cultural background, and past experiences. For some women, beards may evoke feelings of admiration, desire, and fascination, while for others, they may be seen as unappealing or even intimidating.

Furthermore, the appeal of beards to women may also be influenced by psychological factors such as the "mere-exposure effect" and the "contrast effect." The mere-exposure effect suggests that repeated exposure to a stimulus, such as facial hair, can lead to increased familiarity and liking over time. Similarly, the contrast effect posits that positive attributes associated with beards, such as masculinity and confidence, can enhance perceptions of attractiveness when compared to individuals without facial hair.

In addition to cultural and psychological influences, media representation and celebrity culture also shape women's perceptions of beards and their attractiveness. In recent years, beards have experienced a resurgence in popularity, with many celebrities and public figures sporting facial hair as a fashion statement. This increased visibility of beards in the media has helped to normalize and even glamorize facial hair, influencing women's perceptions of attractiveness and desirability.

Despite the diversity of preferences when it comes to facial hair, research suggests that women's attraction to beards may be influenced by factors such as facial symmetry, grooming habits, and overall facial aesthetics. While some women may prefer clean-shaven faces, others may find the rugged charm and masculinity of beards irresistible.

Overall, the psychology of beards from a woman's perspective is a multifaceted phenomenon that reflects a combination of biological, cultural, and psychological factors. While evolutionary instincts may play a role in women's attraction to facial hair, individual preferences, cultural influences, and personal experiences also shape perceptions of attractiveness and desirability. As such, the appeal of beards to women remains a fascinating area of study that offers valuable insights into the complexities of human attraction and the role of facial hair in shaping romantic relationships.

Beards and perceived health: The male perspective

The perception of health in relation to beards is a topic that has garnered considerable attention, particularly from the male perspective. While facial hair has long been associated with masculinity and attractiveness, its impact on perceived health is a subject of ongoing debate and investigation.

From a male perspective, beards are often perceived as a symbol of vitality, strength, and ruggedness. Many men view facial hair as a natural expression of their masculinity and may believe that sporting a beard enhances their overall appearance and conveys an image of robust health. Indeed, throughout history, beards have been associated with qualities such as wisdom, maturity, and physical prowess, contributing to their perceived appeal among men.

However, the relationship between beards and perceived health is complex and can be influenced by a variety of factors. One such factor is grooming habits and maintenance practices. Well-groomed beards that are clean, trimmed, and neatly styled are generally perceived as more attractive and hygienic than unkempt or unruly facial hair. Men who take pride in their grooming routines may be perceived as more health-conscious and attentive to personal hygiene, which can enhance their overall attractiveness and perceived health.

Additionally, cultural and societal norms play a significant role in shaping perceptions of beards and their association with health. In some cultures, beards are revered as a symbol of strength, wisdom, and spiritual enlightenment, with men often growing facial hair as a sign of religious devotion or cultural identity. As such, individuals from these cultural backgrounds may view beards as indicative of good health and spiritual well-being, further reinforcing positive associations between facial hair and perceived health.

Moreover, evolutionary theories suggest that facial hair may serve as a secondary sexual characteristic that signals reproductive fitness and genetic quality. According to this perspective, men with full, well-developed beards may be perceived as healthier and more virile, as facial hair growth is influenced by testosterone levels and other hormonal factors. From a male perspective, growing a beard may be seen as a way to assert one's masculinity and signal reproductive potential, thereby enhancing perceptions of health and attractiveness.

However, it is essential to recognize that perceptions of health in relation to beards can vary widely among individuals and may be influenced by personal preferences, cultural beliefs, and societal norms. While some men may view facial hair as a positive attribute that enhances their perceived health and attractiveness, others may have different opinions based on their own experiences and cultural backgrounds.

Furthermore, research on the hygiene implications of beards has yielded mixed findings, with some studies suggesting that beards may harbor bacteria and other microorganisms that could potentially pose health risks. While proper grooming and hygiene practices can mitigate these concerns to some extent, individuals with certain medical conditions or compromised immune systems may need to take extra precautions when maintaining facial hair.

In conclusion, the perception of health in relation to beards is a multifaceted phenomenon that reflects a combination of biological, cultural, and social factors. While facial hair has long been associated with masculinity and attractiveness, its impact on perceived health varies among individuals and may be influenced by grooming habits, cultural beliefs, and societal norms. As such, the psychology of beards from a male perspective offers valuable insights into the complexities of human perception and the role of facial hair in shaping perceptions of health and attractiveness.

Beard Envy & Beard Mockery: The Inter-beard Dynamics

Beard envy and beard mockery represent two contrasting dynamics within the realm of facial hair perception and social interaction. While some individuals may envy those with impressive beards, others may engage in mockery or ridicule, reflecting a complex interplay of psychological, social, and cultural factors.

Beard envy arises from a desire to possess the attributes associated with facial hair, such as masculinity, maturity, and attractiveness. For some individuals, observing others with full, well-groomed beards may evoke feelings of admiration and aspiration, leading to a sense of longing or envy. This phenomenon is particularly prevalent among men who struggle to grow facial hair or who perceive themselves as lacking in masculinity compared to their bearded counterparts.

Moreover, societal ideals of masculinity and attractiveness often prioritize the presence of facial hair, further fueling feelings of beard envy among individuals who do not conform to these standards. In contemporary culture, beards are frequently portrayed as symbols of ruggedness, virility, and confidence, leading many men to covet the perceived benefits associated with facial hair.

Conversely, beard mockery involves the ridicule or belittlement of individuals based on their facial hair or lack thereof. This behavior may stem from insecurities, social norms, or cultural stereotypes that associate certain facial hair styles with negative attributes such as unkemptness, laziness, or lack of professionalism. Individuals who engage in beard mockery may use derogatory remarks, jokes, or gestures to mock or demean those with facial hair, perpetuating harmful stereotypes and reinforcing societal ideals of masculinity and attractiveness.

The interplay between beard envy and beard mockery highlights the complex dynamics of social comparison and identity formation within the context of facial hair. While some individuals may experience envy towards those with impressive beards, others may resort to mockery as a means of asserting their own sense of superiority or conformity to social norms.

Moreover, the prevalence of beard envy and beard mockery underscores the significance of facial hair in shaping perceptions of masculinity and attractiveness. In a society where physical appearance is often equated with social status and desirability, the presence or absence of facial hair can have profound implications for how individuals are perceived and treated by others.

It is essential to recognize that both beard envy and beard mockery can have negative consequences for individuals' self-esteem, mental well-being, and social interactions. Those who experience beard envy may struggle with feelings of inadequacy or self-doubt, while those subjected to beard mockery may face discrimination or marginalization based on their appearance.

In conclusion, beard envy and beard mockery represent two distinct yet interconnected dynamics within the realm of facial hair perception and social interaction. While beard envy reflects a desire to possess the attributes associated with facial hair, beard mockery involves the ridicule or belittlement of individuals based on their facial hair or lack thereof. Understanding these dynamics can provide valuable insights into the complexities of human behavior, social dynamics, and identity formation within the context of facial hair.

Beard wars: Envy and derision

Beard wars, characterized by envy and derision, epitomize the multifaceted nature of societal perceptions surrounding facial hair. This phenomenon underscores the interplay of psychological, cultural, and social factors that influence how individuals perceive and respond to facial hair, particularly in the context of masculinity, attractiveness, and social status.

At the heart of beard wars lies the phenomenon of beard envy, wherein individuals harbor feelings of longing or admiration towards those with impressive facial hair. Beard envy often stems from societal ideals of masculinity and attractiveness, which equate the presence of a full, well-groomed beard with ruggedness, virility, and confidence. As a result, individuals who are unable to grow facial hair or do not conform to these standards may experience feelings of inadequacy or envy towards their bearded counterparts.

Conversely, beard derision represents the flip side of the coin, characterized by mockery or ridicule directed towards individuals based on their facial hair or lack thereof. This behavior may arise from deeply ingrained cultural stereotypes or social norms that associate certain facial hair styles with negative attributes such as unkemptness, laziness, or lack of professionalism. Those who engage in beard derision may use derogatory remarks, jokes, or gestures to belittle or demean individuals with facial hair, perpetuating harmful stereotypes and reinforcing societal ideals of masculinity and attractiveness.

The dynamics of beard wars are further complicated by factors such as personal insecurities, social comparison, and peer pressure. Individuals may feel compelled to conform to societal expectations regarding facial hair, leading to feelings of envy towards those who possess desirable beard traits. Conversely, those who do not fit the mold may become targets of derision or mockery, further exacerbating feelings of insecurity or inadequacy.

Moreover, the advent of social media and digital culture has amplified the phenomenon of beard wars, providing a platform for individuals to showcase their facial hair and engage in online communities centered around beard culture. On one hand, social media has fostered a sense of camaraderie and mutual admiration among beard enthusiasts, allowing individuals to connect and share tips, grooming techniques, and style inspiration. On the other hand, it has also facilitated the spread of harmful stereotypes and beauty standards, perpetuating unrealistic ideals of masculinity and attractiveness.

The consequences of beard wars extend beyond individual self-esteem to encompass broader societal attitudes towards facial hair and gender expression. By perpetuating stereotypes and reinforcing narrow definitions of masculinity, beard wars contribute to the marginalization and discrimination of individuals who do not conform to traditional gender norms or beauty standards.

In conclusion, beard wars epitomize the complex interplay of psychological, cultural, and social factors that shape perceptions surrounding facial hair. While beard envy reflects a desire to possess the attributes associated with facial hair, beard derision represents the ridicule or belittlement of individuals based on their appearance. Understanding the underlying dynamics of beard wars can provide valuable insights into the complexities of human behavior, social dynamics, and identity formation within the context of facial hair.

Confronting beard mockery: Psychological strategies

Confronting beard mockery requires a multifaceted approach that incorporates psychological strategies aimed at promoting self-confidence, resilience, and assertiveness. In the face of derogatory remarks or ridicule, individuals with facial hair can employ various techniques to mitigate the impact of beard mockery and maintain a positive self-image.

One effective psychological strategy for confronting beard mockery is reframing negative self-talk and challenging internalized stereotypes. Individuals who experience beard mockery may internalize negative beliefs about themselves or their appearance, leading to feelings of insecurity or self-doubt. By actively challenging these beliefs and reframing negative self-talk, individuals can cultivate a more positive self-image and develop resilience in the face of criticism.

Cognitive-behavioral techniques, such as cognitive restructuring and positive self-talk, can be particularly helpful in this regard. Cognitive restructuring involves identifying and challenging irrational or negative thoughts related to facial hair and replacing them with more realistic and positive beliefs. Similarly, positive self-talk involves consciously replacing self-critical or derogatory thoughts with affirming and empowering statements, thereby bolstering self-esteem and confidence.

Another important psychological strategy for confronting beard mockery is assertiveness training, which involves learning how to assert one's rights, needs, and boundaries in a respectful and confident manner. Assertiveness training can help individuals develop effective communication skills and assert their worth and dignity in the face of criticism or ridicule. By learning how to express themselves assertively and set clear boundaries, individuals can assert control over how they are treated and perceived by others.

Furthermore, building a strong social support network can provide invaluable psychological resources for confronting beard mockery. Surrounding oneself with supportive friends, family members, or peers who accept and validate one's appearance can help buffer the negative impact of beard mockery and foster a sense of belonging and acceptance. Additionally, seeking out online or community-based support groups for individuals with facial hair can provide a sense of camaraderie and solidarity, allowing individuals to share experiences, seek advice, and receive validation from others who understand their unique challenges.

In addition to individual-level strategies, addressing beard mockery also requires broader societal efforts to challenge stereotypes and promote inclusivity and acceptance of diverse appearances. Educating others about the harmful effects of stereotypes and discrimination based on appearance can help raise awareness and foster empathy and understanding. Additionally, advocating for policies and initiatives that promote diversity and inclusivity in workplaces, schools, and communities can help create environments where individuals feel valued and respected regardless of their appearance.

Ultimately, confronting beard mockery requires a combination of individual and societal-level strategies aimed at promoting self-confidence, resilience, and inclusivity. By employing psychological techniques such as cognitive restructuring, assertiveness training, and social support, individuals can assert control over how they are perceived and treated by others and cultivate a positive self-image in the face of beard mockery. Moreover, by challenging stereotypes and advocating for greater acceptance and inclusivity, we can create a society where individuals are valued for their unique qualities and appearances.

The Fear of Beards: Pogonophobia Explored

Pogonophobia, or the fear of beards, is a relatively uncommon yet fascinating psychological phenomenon that can have significant implications for individuals who experience it. While some may view beards as symbols of masculinity, wisdom, or personal style, others may find them intimidating or unsettling. Understanding the psychology behind pogonophobia can shed light on the underlying factors that contribute to this fear and how it manifests in different individuals.

One possible explanation for pogonophobia is rooted in evolutionary psychology. Throughout human history, facial hair has been associated with masculinity and sexual maturity, signaling traits such as strength, dominance, and reproductive fitness. In ancestral environments, individuals with prominent facial hair may have been perceived as more formidable or threatening to rivals, leading to a natural aversion or fear response in some individuals. This evolutionary predisposition towards associating beards with dominance or aggression could contribute to the development of pogonophobia in certain individuals.

Additionally, cultural and social factors play a significant role in shaping attitudes towards facial hair and may influence the development of pogonophobia. In some cultures or subcultures, beards may be associated with specific stereotypes or stigmas, such as uncleanliness, nonconformity, or criminality. Exposure to negative portrayals of individuals with beards in media or popular culture could reinforce these stereotypes and contribute to the development of fear or aversion towards facial hair. Furthermore, social experiences, such as negative interactions with individuals who have beards or witnessing aggressive behavior from individuals with facial hair, may also contribute to the development of pogonophobia.

Psychological theories related to fear and anxiety can also provide insights into the mechanisms underlying pogonophobia. For example, classical conditioning, a concept pioneered by psychologist Ivan Pavlov, suggests that phobias can develop through associative learning processes. In the case of pogonophobia, a negative or traumatic experience involving someone with facial hair, such as intimidation or aggression, could become associated with the sight or presence of beards, leading to an irrational fear response in similar situations.

Moreover, cognitive-behavioral theories of anxiety highlight the role of cognitive biases and distorted thinking patterns in the maintenance of phobias. Individuals with pogonophobia may engage in cognitive processes such as selective attention, where they disproportionately focus on threatening or negative aspects of facial hair while discounting contradictory information. Additionally, catastrophic thinking, or the tendency to imagine the worst-case scenarios, may exacerbate feelings of fear or anxiety related to beards, leading to avoidance behaviors or exaggerated reactions in the presence of facial hair.

In terms of treatment, individuals experiencing pogonophobia may benefit from cognitive-behavioral therapy (CBT), a well-established therapeutic approach for addressing phobias and anxiety disorders. CBT techniques such as exposure therapy, where individuals gradually confront their fears in a controlled manner, can help desensitize individuals to the sight or presence of beards and reduce anxiety responses over time. Additionally, cognitive restructuring techniques can help individuals challenge and modify irrational beliefs or thought patterns related to beards, leading to a more balanced and realistic perspective.

In conclusion, pogonophobia is a complex psychological phenomenon that can arise from a combination of evolutionary, cultural, and cognitive factors. By understanding the underlying mechanisms of pogonophobia and employing evidence-based treatments such as cognitive-behavioral therapy, individuals experiencing fear or anxiety related to beards can learn to manage their symptoms and lead fulfilling lives free from the constraints of phobia.

What is Pogonophobia?

Pogonophobia is a psychological condition characterized by an irrational and persistent fear or aversion towards beards. Derived from the Greek word "pogon," meaning beard, and "phobos," meaning fear, pogonophobia can manifest in various ways, ranging from mild discomfort or anxiety in the presence of bearded individuals to severe panic attacks or avoidance behaviors.

The origins of pogonophobia can be traced back to a combination of evolutionary, cultural, and psychological factors. From an evolutionary perspective, facial hair, particularly in males, has long been associated with traits such as masculinity, dominance, and maturity. Throughout human history, individuals with prominent facial hair may have been perceived as more formidable or intimidating, leading to a natural aversion or fear response in some individuals. This evolutionary predisposition towards associating beards with dominance or aggression could contribute to the development of pogonophobia in certain individuals.

Cultural and social factors also play a significant role in shaping attitudes towards facial hair and may influence the development of pogonophobia. In some cultures or subcultures, beards may be associated with specific stereotypes or stigmas, such as uncleanliness, nonconformity, or criminality. Exposure to negative portrayals of individuals with beards in media or popular culture could reinforce these stereotypes and contribute to the development of fear or aversion towards facial hair. Furthermore, social experiences, such as negative interactions with individuals who have beards or witnessing aggressive behavior from individuals with facial hair, may also contribute to the development of pogonophobia.

Psychological theories related to fear and anxiety can further elucidate the mechanisms underlying pogonophobia. Classical conditioning, a concept pioneered by psychologist Ivan Pavlov, suggests that phobias can develop through associative learning processes. In the case of pogonophobia, a negative or traumatic experience involving someone with facial hair, such as intimidation or aggression, could become associated with the sight or presence of beards, leading to an irrational fear response in similar situations.

Cognitive-behavioral theories of anxiety highlight the role of cognitive biases and distorted thinking patterns in the maintenance of phobias. Individuals with pogonophobia may engage in cognitive processes such as selective attention, where they disproportionately focus on threatening or negative aspects of facial hair while discounting contradictory information. Additionally, catastrophic thinking, or the tendency to imagine the worst-case scenarios, may exacerbate feelings of fear or anxiety related to beards, leading to avoidance behaviors or exaggerated reactions in the presence of facial hair.

In terms of treatment, individuals experiencing pogonophobia may benefit from cognitive-behavioral therapy (CBT), a well-established therapeutic approach for addressing phobias and anxiety disorders. CBT techniques such as exposure therapy, where individuals gradually confront their fears in a controlled manner, can help desensitize individuals to the sight or presence of beards and reduce anxiety responses over time. Additionally, cognitive restructuring techniques can help individuals challenge and modify irrational beliefs or thought patterns related to beards, leading to a more balanced and realistic perspective.

In conclusion, pogonophobia is a complex psychological phenomenon that can arise from a combination of evolutionary, cultural, and cognitive factors. By understanding the underlying mechanisms of pogonophobia and employing evidence-based treatments such as cognitive-behavioral therapy, individuals experiencing fear or anxiety related to beards can learn to manage their symptoms and lead fulfilling lives free from the constraints of phobia.

Coping with beard-related fear

Coping with beard-related fear, also known as pogonophobia, can be a challenging journey for individuals experiencing anxiety or discomfort in the presence of facial hair. While pogonophobia may vary in severity from mild unease to debilitating panic attacks, there are several coping strategies and techniques that individuals can employ to manage their fear and improve their quality of life.

One of the most effective coping strategies for pogonophobia is exposure therapy, a form of cognitive-behavioral therapy (CBT) that involves gradually exposing individuals to the source of their fear in a controlled and systematic manner. In the case of beard-related fear, exposure therapy may involve starting with less intimidating stimuli, such as looking at pictures of people with beards or watching videos featuring individuals with facial hair. Over time, individuals can progress to more challenging exposure exercises, such as being in the presence of someone with a beard or touching a beard themselves. Through repeated exposure and practice, individuals can learn to tolerate and eventually overcome their fear of beards.

Mindfulness-based techniques, such as deep breathing exercises and meditation, can also be helpful in coping with beard-related fear. By focusing on the present moment and engaging in relaxation exercises, individuals can reduce feelings of anxiety and stress associated with encountering facial hair. Techniques such as progressive muscle relaxation, where individuals systematically tense and then relax different muscle groups in the body, can help alleviate physical tension and promote a sense of calmness and relaxation.

Cognitive restructuring, another CBT technique, involves identifying and challenging irrational thoughts or beliefs related to beards and replacing them with more balanced and realistic perspectives. For example, individuals with pogonophobia may have negative or exaggerated beliefs about the dangers or threats posed by individuals with facial hair. Through cognitive restructuring, individuals can learn to recognize and challenge these irrational beliefs, leading to a reduction in fear and anxiety.

Social support can also play a crucial role in coping with beard-related fear. Talking to friends, family members, or support groups about their experiences and feelings can provide individuals with validation, encouragement, and practical advice for managing their fear. Supportive relationships can also serve as a source of comfort and reassurance during challenging times, helping individuals feel less isolated and alone in their struggles.

In some cases, seeking professional help from a therapist or mental health professional may be necessary to effectively cope with pogonophobia. Therapists trained in CBT techniques can provide personalized treatment plans tailored to the individual's specific needs and circumstances. Additionally, therapists can help individuals explore the underlying factors contributing to their fear of beards and develop coping skills to manage their symptoms more effectively.

It's important to remember that coping with pogonophobia is a gradual process that may take time and patience. It's okay to seek support from others and to take things at your own pace. With persistence, self-care, and the support of loved ones and mental health professionals, individuals can learn to effectively cope with beard-related fear and lead fulfilling lives free from the constraints of phobia.

Beardless Men in a Bearded World

Living as a beardless man in a world where beards are often celebrated and admired can present unique challenges and experiences. While some individuals may embrace their smooth-faced appearance with confidence, others may grapple with feelings of insecurity, inadequacy, or even exclusion in a society that values facial hair as a symbol of masculinity and attractiveness.

For many beardless men, societal expectations and cultural norms surrounding masculinity and grooming can contribute to feelings of pressure or self-consciousness. In a world where beards are often associated with traits such as strength, maturity, and ruggedness, individuals without facial hair may worry about not measuring up to these ideals or being perceived as less masculine. This pressure to conform to traditional standards of masculinity can lead to feelings of insecurity or inadequacy among beardless men, impacting their self-esteem and overall well-being.

In addition to concerns about masculinity, beardless men may also face social stigma or teasing from others who view facial hair as a desirable or attractive trait. Whether it's playful banter among friends or more overt forms of ridicule, beardless men may find themselves the target of jokes or comments about their lack of facial hair. This teasing or mockery can further exacerbate feelings of self-consciousness or insecurity, causing individuals to feel alienated or excluded from certain social circles or activities.

Despite these challenges, many beardless men find ways to embrace and celebrate their smooth-faced appearance. Some may cultivate alternative forms of self-expression or identity, such as through fashion, grooming, or personal interests, that allow them to feel confident and comfortable in their own skin. Others may find strength in forging connections with like-minded individuals who share similar experiences or perspectives, creating a sense of community and belonging outside of traditional notions of masculinity.

Furthermore, it's important to recognize that the value of a person extends far beyond their physical appearance or adherence to societal norms. While facial hair may be perceived as a symbol of masculinity in some cultures or contexts, true masculinity is defined by qualities such as compassion, integrity, and resilience, which are not contingent upon the presence of facial hair. By focusing on their inner strengths and values, beardless men can cultivate a sense of self-worth and confidence that transcends superficial notions of attractiveness or masculinity.

Ultimately, the experience of being a beardless man in a bearded world is as diverse and varied as the individuals who inhabit it. While some may struggle with feelings of insecurity or social pressure, others may embrace their smooth-faced appearance with pride and confidence. By challenging traditional notions of masculinity and embracing a more inclusive and accepting definition of beauty and identity, society can create a more supportive and empowering environment for all individuals, regardless of their facial hair status. Whether bearded or beardless, every person deserves to feel valued, respected, and accepted for who they are.

The stigma of the 'bare-faced'

In a society where beards are often regarded as symbols of masculinity, maturity, and attractiveness, those who lack facial hair can sometimes find themselves subject to stigma or scrutiny. Referred to as the "bare-faced" or "clean-shaven," individuals without beards may experience social pressure or judgment due to their smooth-faced appearance.

The stigma surrounding the "bare-faced" can be attributed to various factors, including cultural norms, media representations, and personal perceptions of masculinity. From ancient civilizations to modern-day pop culture, beards have been associated with traits such as wisdom, strength, and virility, leading to their widespread admiration and emulation. Consequently, those who do not conform to this idealized image of masculinity may be perceived as lacking in these qualities, facing discrimination or marginalization as a result.

Media representations play a significant role in perpetuating the stigma of the "bare-faced." In movies, television shows, and advertisements, bearded men are often portrayed as rugged, charismatic, and desirable, while clean-shaven men may be relegated to roles that are less prominent or authoritative. These depictions reinforce the notion that facial hair is synonymous with masculinity and attractiveness, further marginalizing those who do not possess it.

Personal perceptions of masculinity also contribute to the stigma of the "bare-faced." In many cultures, men are socialized to believe that facial hair is a natural and essential aspect of their identity, symbolizing maturity, authority, and sexual prowess. As a result, individuals without beards may internalize feelings of inadequacy or inferiority, comparing themselves unfavorably to their bearded counterparts and seeking validation through conformity to traditional masculine norms.

The stigma of the "bare-faced" can manifest in various ways, from subtle forms of social exclusion to overt acts of ridicule or discrimination. In social settings, clean-shaven individuals may feel pressured to conform to masculine ideals by growing facial hair or resorting to other forms of grooming and self-presentation. Failure to adhere to these norms may result in feelings of insecurity, self-doubt, or social ostracism, as individuals without beards may be perceived as less competent, attractive, or desirable by their peers.

Moreover, the stigma of the "bare-faced" can have profound effects on an individual's self-esteem and psychological well-being. Studies have shown that men who do not conform to traditional standards of masculinity may experience higher levels of stress, anxiety, and depression, as they grapple with societal expectations and internalized stereotypes about what it means to be a man. Additionally, the stigma of the "bare-faced" may contribute to feelings of social isolation or alienation, as individuals without beards may struggle to fit in or find acceptance within their peer groups or communities.

In conclusion, the stigma of the "bare-faced" reflects broader societal attitudes towards masculinity, appearance, and identity. While facial hair is often celebrated and admired as a symbol of masculinity and attractiveness, those who lack beards may face social pressure, judgment, or discrimination due to their smooth-faced appearance. By challenging traditional notions of masculinity and promoting greater acceptance and inclusivity, society can create a more supportive and empowering environment for all individuals, regardless of their facial hair status.

Overcoming beard inferiority complex

The phenomenon of the "beard inferiority complex" refers to the feelings of inadequacy, insecurity, or self-doubt experienced by individuals who perceive themselves as less masculine or attractive due to their lack of facial hair. While societal norms and media representations often idealize beards as symbols of masculinity and virility, not everyone can grow or maintain facial hair to the same extent. As a result, those who do not conform to this standard may experience feelings of inferiority or self-consciousness, struggling to reconcile their appearance with societal expectations of masculinity.

One of the first steps in overcoming the beard inferiority complex is to challenge societal norms and stereotypes surrounding masculinity and appearance. It is essential to recognize that there is no one-size-fits-all definition of masculinity and that facial hair does not determine a person's worth or identity. By questioning traditional notions of masculinity and embracing diverse expressions of gender and identity, individuals can begin to dismantle the internalized beliefs that contribute to the beard inferiority complex.

Another important aspect of overcoming the beard inferiority complex is cultivating self-confidence and self-acceptance. Rather than seeking validation from external sources or conforming to societal standards, individuals should focus on developing a positive self-image and embracing their unique qualities and attributes. By practicing self-care, setting realistic goals, and celebrating their achievements, individuals can build resilience and confidence in themselves, regardless of their facial hair status.

Furthermore, it can be helpful for individuals struggling with the beard inferiority complex to reframe their perspective on masculinity and attractiveness. Instead of viewing facial hair as the sole determinant of masculinity, individuals can explore other aspects of their identity, such as their personality, values, and interests, that contribute to their sense of self. By broadening their definition of masculinity and embracing a more inclusive and diverse understanding of attractiveness, individuals can liberate themselves from the constraints of societal expectations and find greater fulfillment and happiness in their lives.

Additionally, seeking support from friends, family members, or mental health professionals can be instrumental in overcoming the beard inferiority complex. Opening up about feelings of insecurity or self-doubt can help individuals gain perspective, receive validation, and develop coping strategies for managing negative thoughts and emotions. Therapy, support groups, or online communities can provide a safe space for individuals to explore their feelings, share their experiences, and receive encouragement and advice from others who may be facing similar challenges.

Finally, it is essential for individuals struggling with the beard inferiority complex to practice self-compassion and kindness towards themselves. Rather than criticizing or judging themselves for perceived shortcomings or inadequacies, individuals should practice self-acceptance and self-love, recognizing that they are worthy and deserving of respect and admiration, regardless of their appearance. By cultivating a sense of compassion and understanding towards themselves, individuals can overcome the beard inferiority complex and embrace their authentic selves with confidence and pride.

Beard and Confidence: The Lion's Mane Phenomenon

The Lion's Mane Phenomenon refers to the observed correlation between having a beard and increased confidence in individuals. While this phenomenon may seem anecdotal, there is growing evidence to suggest that the presence of facial hair can indeed influence a person's self-perception and confidence levels.

One reason behind the Lion's Mane Phenomenon is the association between beards and masculinity. Throughout history and across cultures, facial hair has been linked to traits such as strength, wisdom, and authority. As a result, individuals who sport beards may subconsciously internalize these associations, leading them to perceive themselves as more masculine and confident. This sense of masculinity can translate into increased self-assurance and assertiveness in social interactions and professional settings.

Moreover, the act of growing and maintaining a beard requires dedication, patience, and self-discipline. Successfully cultivating a beard can instill a sense of pride and accomplishment in individuals, bolstering their self-esteem and confidence. Additionally, the compliments and positive reactions received from others can further reinforce these feelings, providing external validation for one's appearance and grooming choices.

Furthermore, beards have been shown to enhance facial features and mask perceived imperfections, leading to an overall improvement in self-image and confidence. For some individuals, facial hair can serve as a form of self-expression, allowing them to project a desired image or persona to the world. By carefully grooming and styling their beard, individuals can cultivate a sense of identity and confidence that extends beyond physical appearance.

Additionally, wearing a beard can serve as a form of psychological armor, providing individuals with a sense of security and protection in social situations. The physical presence of facial hair can create a barrier between oneself and others, serving as a buffer against negative judgment or criticism. This perceived sense of protection can empower individuals to express themselves more freely and confidently, without fear of rejection or ridicule.

Furthermore, research has suggested that facial hair may influence how individuals are perceived by others, with bearded individuals often being perceived as more dominant, mature, and competent. These positive perceptions can contribute to an individual's sense of self-worth and confidence, reinforcing the belief that their beard enhances their overall attractiveness and presence.

However, it is essential to recognize that the Lion's Mane Phenomenon is not universal, and the relationship between beards and confidence can vary from person to person. Factors such as personal preferences, cultural norms, and individual differences in facial hair growth patterns can all influence how individuals perceive and experience their beards.

In conclusion, the Lion's Mane Phenomenon highlights the complex interplay between facial hair and confidence in individuals. While the presence of a beard may indeed boost confidence levels for many people, it is essential to recognize that confidence is a multifaceted construct influenced by various factors. Whether or not one chooses to sport a beard, cultivating confidence ultimately involves embracing one's unique identity, strengths, and qualities, regardless of external appearance.

The boost of self-esteem from growing a beard

Growing a beard can be a transformative experience for many individuals, providing a significant boost to their self-esteem and confidence. While the decision to grow a beard is often influenced by personal preferences and cultural norms, the psychological benefits associated with facial hair growth are undeniable.

One reason why growing a beard can boost self-esteem is the sense of achievement and control it provides. For many individuals, the process of growing and maintaining a beard requires patience, dedication, and perseverance. As the beard gradually takes shape, individuals can take pride in their ability to cultivate and shape their appearance according to their preferences. This sense of mastery over one's physical appearance can foster a profound sense of accomplishment and self-efficacy, boosting self-esteem in the process.

Moreover, growing a beard can enhance feelings of masculinity and identity for many individuals. Throughout history and across cultures, facial hair has been associated with traits such as strength, wisdom, and virility. By growing a beard, individuals can tap into these cultural associations, aligning themselves with a traditional symbol of masculinity. This alignment can lead to a heightened sense of self-confidence and empowerment, as individuals feel more connected to their gender identity and societal expectations of masculinity.

Furthermore, facial hair can serve as a form of self-expression, allowing individuals to showcase their personality and individuality to the world. The style, length, and grooming of a beard can convey unique messages about an individual's values, interests, and lifestyle choices. By carefully curating their facial hair, individuals can assert their identity and assertiveness, leading to increased self-esteem and confidence.

Additionally, the positive feedback and reactions received from others can further reinforce feelings of self-worth and confidence in individuals with beards. Compliments on one's facial hair can serve as a form of validation, affirming that their grooming choices are appreciated and admired by others. This external validation can bolster self-esteem and confidence, providing individuals with a sense of social acceptance and approval.

Moreover, growing a beard can enhance facial features and mask perceived imperfections, leading to an overall improvement in self-image and confidence. For some individuals, facial hair can serve as a form of camouflage, concealing blemishes, scars, or asymmetries on the face. By framing the face and drawing attention away from perceived flaws, a well-groomed beard can enhance facial aesthetics and boost self-esteem.

Furthermore, research has shown that facial hair can influence how individuals are perceived by others, with bearded individuals often being perceived as more dominant, mature, and competent. These positive perceptions can translate into increased self-confidence and self-assurance, as individuals internalize the positive feedback and reactions they receive from others.

In conclusion, growing a beard can provide a significant boost to self-esteem and confidence for many individuals. The process of cultivating facial hair can foster feelings of achievement, masculinity, and self-expression, while positive feedback from others can further reinforce these feelings. Ultimately, the decision to grow a beard is a deeply personal one, but for many, it represents a powerful tool for enhancing self-esteem and confidence in oneself.

Maintaining the confidence: Keeping the beard groomed

Maintaining a well-groomed beard is not just about aesthetics; it's also about preserving the confidence and positive self-image that come with having facial hair. While growing a beard can be a transformative experience for many individuals, neglecting its maintenance can have adverse effects on one's confidence and self-esteem.

First and foremost, proper grooming is essential for ensuring that a beard looks neat, tidy, and well-maintained. A scraggly, unkempt beard can give off an impression of laziness or lack of self-care, which may undermine the confidence that comes with having facial hair. Regular trimming, shaping, and cleaning are essential for keeping a beard looking its best and projecting an image of confidence and professionalism.

Furthermore, maintaining a groomed beard can help individuals feel more in control of their appearance and grooming habits. By dedicating time and effort to grooming their facial hair, individuals demonstrate a commitment to self-care and personal presentation, which can contribute to a sense of pride and self-respect. Taking ownership of one's grooming routine can instill a sense of confidence and empowerment, as individuals actively shape their external image to align with their desired self-image.

Additionally, proper beard maintenance can enhance feelings of masculinity and identity for many individuals. A well-groomed beard can serve as a symbol of strength, maturity, and virility, reinforcing traditional notions of masculinity and identity. By ensuring that their facial hair looks clean, healthy, and well-kept, individuals can project an image of confidence and assertiveness that aligns with societal expectations of masculinity.

Moreover, grooming a beard can be a form of self-expression and individuality, allowing individuals to showcase their personality and style preferences. The style, length, and grooming of a beard can convey unique messages about an individual's values, interests, and lifestyle choices. By carefully grooming their facial hair, individuals can assert their identity and creativity, projecting an image of confidence and authenticity to the world.

Furthermore, maintaining a groomed beard can lead to positive interactions and perceptions from others, which can further bolster feelings of confidence and self-esteem. A well-groomed beard is often seen as a sign of good hygiene, self-care, and attention to detail, which can elicit admiration and respect from peers, colleagues, and strangers alike.

Positive feedback and compliments on one's facial hair can serve as a form of validation, affirming that their grooming efforts are noticed and appreciated by others.

In conclusion, maintaining a well-groomed beard is essential for preserving the confidence and positive self-image that come with having facial hair. Proper grooming not only ensures that a beard looks neat and tidy but also reinforces feelings of control, masculinity, and individuality. By dedicating time and effort to grooming their facial hair, individuals can project an image of confidence, professionalism, and self-respect that aligns with their desired self-image.

Rise of the Bearded Stereotype: Media's Influence

The portrayal of bearded individuals in media has played a significant role in shaping societal perceptions and stereotypes surrounding facial hair. From movies and television shows to advertisements and social media, the media has often depicted bearded men in specific roles and character archetypes, contributing to the rise of the bearded stereotype.

One common stereotype perpetuated by the media is the association of beards with ruggedness, masculinity, and strength. Bearded characters are often portrayed as tough, rugged, and capable, embodying traditional ideals of masculinity and virility. This stereotype can be traced back to the portrayal of bearded figures in popular culture, such as rugged action heroes or stoic warriors, who exude confidence and power through their facial hair.

Moreover, the media has also perpetuated stereotypes linking beards to rebellion, nonconformity, and counterculture. Bearded characters are often depicted as rebels or outsiders, challenging societal norms and conventions through their refusal to conform to clean-shaven standards of appearance. This stereotype is evident in the portrayal of bearded characters in films, television shows, and advertisements as free-spirited, independent individuals who reject mainstream ideals of beauty and grooming.

Additionally, the media has contributed to the association of beards with wisdom, intellect, and authority. Bearded characters are often portrayed as wise mentors, intellectuals, or authority figures, whose facial hair symbolizes their experience, knowledge, and leadership. This stereotype is evident in the depiction of bearded professors, scientists, or wise old men in literature, film, and television, who are revered for their wisdom and insight.

Furthermore, the media has perpetuated stereotypes associating beards with certain personality traits or lifestyle choices. Bearded individuals are often depicted as outdoorsy, adventurous, or rugged, with their facial hair serving as a symbol of their adventurous spirit and connection to nature. This stereotype is evident in the portrayal of bearded characters in outdoor and adventure-themed media, where facial hair is often associated with a love of the outdoors and an adventurous lifestyle.

However, it is essential to recognize that these stereotypes are not always accurate or representative of all individuals with beards. While some bearded individuals may embody these stereotypes, many others do not fit neatly into these categories. Beards come in all shapes, sizes, and styles, and individuals choose to grow facial hair for a variety of reasons that may not align with these stereotypes.

Moreover, the media's portrayal of beards can also have real-world implications for individuals who choose to grow facial hair. For example, individuals with beards may face discrimination or prejudice in certain contexts, such as the workplace, where clean-shaven standards of appearance may be enforced. Additionally, the media's perpetuation of certain stereotypes surrounding beards can influence societal attitudes and perceptions toward individuals with facial hair, leading to stereotyping and stigmatization.

In conclusion, the media plays a significant role in shaping societal perceptions and stereotypes surrounding beards. From rugged action heroes to wise mentors, the media has perpetuated various stereotypes associating beards with masculinity, rebellion, wisdom, and adventure. While these stereotypes may not always accurately reflect the diversity of individuals with beards, they can have real-world implications for how bearded individuals are perceived and treated in society.

Beards in Hollywood: Hero or villain?

Beards in Hollywood have been utilized to convey a wide range of character traits, often serving as visual cues to help audiences quickly identify and understand the roles that characters play within a narrative. However, whether a beard is associated with a hero or a villain largely depends on how it is portrayed and contextualized within the story.

In many cases, beards have been used to signify strength, wisdom, and moral integrity, leading to their association with heroic characters. Heroes with beards are often depicted as wise mentors, valiant warriors, or noble leaders who embody traditional ideals of masculinity and honor. For example, iconic characters like Gandalf from "The Lord of the Rings" series and Dumbledore from the "Harry Potter" franchise are both depicted with long, flowing beards that symbolize their wisdom, authority, and benevolence. Similarly, characters like Captain America and Thor from the Marvel Cinematic Universe are portrayed with rugged stubble or neatly trimmed beards, reflecting their strength, resilience, and determination in the face of adversity.

On the other hand, beards have also been used to signify villainy, rebellion, and untrustworthiness in Hollywood films. Villains with beards are often depicted as sinister, manipulative, or morally ambiguous characters who challenge societal norms and conventions. These characters may have unkempt or wild beards, symbolizing their disregard for authority and social order. For example, iconic villains like Darth Vader from "Star Wars" and Jafar from "Aladdin" are both depicted with dark, menacing beards that reflect their malevolent intentions and lust for power. Similarly, characters like Hades from Disney's "Hercules" and Scar from "The Lion King" are portrayed with thin, pointed beards that emphasize their cunning and deceitful nature.

However, it is essential to recognize that the portrayal of beards in Hollywood is not always black and white. While some films may lean into traditional stereotypes by associating beards with heroism or villainy, others may subvert these expectations by portraying complex, multidimensional characters with beards who defy easy categorization. Additionally, the meaning and symbolism of a beard can vary depending on cultural and historical contexts, further complicating its portrayal in film and media.

Furthermore, the perception of beards in Hollywood may also be influenced by changing societal attitudes and trends. In recent years, there has been a resurgence of interest in beards as symbols of masculinity, individuality, and self-expression, leading to a more diverse and nuanced portrayal of facial hair in film and television. As a result, filmmakers and storytellers may be more inclined to challenge traditional stereotypes and explore the complexities of bearded characters in their narratives.

In conclusion, the portrayal of beards in Hollywood is a complex and multifaceted phenomenon that reflects broader cultural attitudes and trends. While beards have often been used to signify heroism or villainy in film and media, their meaning and symbolism can vary depending on the context in which they are presented. As societal attitudes toward facial hair continue to evolve, so too will the portrayal of bearded characters in Hollywood, reflecting the changing dynamics of gender, identity, and representation in popular culture.

Changing stereotypes: Intellectuals with beards

In popular culture, the stereotype of intellectuals with beards has long been ingrained in our collective consciousness. From philosophers and scientists to artists and writers, bearded intellectuals have often been portrayed as wise, knowledgeable, and deeply contemplative individuals. However, this stereotype is not merely a product of fiction or artistic imagination; it has roots in history, psychology, and societal perceptions of masculinity and intelligence.

Historically, beards have been associated with wisdom, intellect, and authority across various cultures and civilizations. In ancient Greece, philosophers like Socrates, Plato, and Aristotle were often depicted with long, flowing beards, symbolizing their intellectual prowess and philosophical depth. Similarly, in the Islamic Golden Age, scholars and scientists like Ibn Sina (Avicenna) and Ibn Khaldun were renowned for their contributions to mathematics, medicine, and philosophy, often sporting prominent beards as a mark of their scholarly status.

In Western society, the association between beards and intellectualism gained traction during the Enlightenment period, a cultural and intellectual movement that emphasized reason, science, and individualism. Philosophers, scientists, and writers of the Enlightenment era, such as Voltaire, Rousseau, and Benjamin Franklin, were often depicted with beards in portraits and illustrations, reflecting their status as intellectuals and proponents of progressive ideas.

Psychologically, the stereotype of intellectuals with beards may be rooted in the concept of "the halo effect," a cognitive bias where individuals perceive others who possess certain traits or characteristics positively across multiple domains. In the case of beards, the association with wisdom, intellect, and authority may lead people to perceive bearded individuals as more intelligent, competent, and trustworthy, regardless of their actual abilities or qualifications. This cognitive bias can influence hiring decisions, social interactions, and overall perceptions of individuals with beards in various contexts.

Furthermore, societal perceptions of masculinity and gender norms play a significant role in shaping the stereotype of intellectuals with beards. Traditionally, masculinity has been associated with traits such as strength, dominance, and assertiveness, while femininity has been associated with traits such as nurturing, empathy, and emotional sensitivity. Beards, with their associations with maturity, virility, and ruggedness, may align more closely with traditional notions of masculinity, leading to their portrayal as symbols of intellectualism and authority.

However, it is essential to recognize that stereotypes are not always accurate reflections of reality. While some intellectuals may choose to grow beards as a personal expression of identity or style, others may prefer to remain clean-shaven or adopt different grooming practices altogether. Additionally, intelligence and wisdom are not determined by physical appearance but rather by a combination of factors such as education, experience, critical thinking skills, and emotional intelligence.

In conclusion, the stereotype of intellectuals with beards reflects historical, psychological, and societal influences on perceptions of masculinity, intelligence, and authority. While this stereotype may have some basis in reality, it is essential to approach it with critical thinking and skepticism, recognizing that individuals should not be judged solely based on their physical appearance. As society continues to evolve, so too will our understanding of the complex interplay between stereotypes, identity, and perception in shaping our views of others.

Beards & Age: The Perception of Wisdom and Years

Throughout history, beards have often been associated with age, wisdom, and experience. The perception of bearded individuals as wise elders is deeply ingrained in many cultures and societies, reflecting broader psychological and societal dynamics related to aging, authority, and respect.

One reason for the association between beards and age is the natural process of facial hair growth. As individuals age, their hair typically becomes coarser and thicker, leading to the development of fuller beards. In many societies, the presence of a beard is often seen as a sign of maturity and wisdom, with older individuals being more likely to sport facial hair than their younger counterparts.

Psychologically, the perception of bearded individuals as wise and experienced may be influenced by cognitive biases such as the "elderly stereotype" and the "halo effect." The elderly stereotype refers to the tendency to associate older individuals with positive attributes such as wisdom, knowledge, and life experience. When combined with the halo effect, which leads people to attribute positive qualities to individuals based on a single characteristic, such as facial hair, the result is a heightened perception of bearded individuals as wise and venerable.

Moreover, societal norms and cultural traditions play a significant role in shaping the perception of beards in relation to age. In many cultures, older men are revered as sources of wisdom and authority, and the presence of a beard serves as a visual symbol of their status as respected elders. This reverence for age and experience is often reflected in religious and cultural traditions, where bearded figures are depicted as wise leaders and spiritual guides.

In addition to perceptions of wisdom and maturity, beards are also associated with masculinity and virility, further enhancing the perception of bearded individuals as authoritative and respected figures. The presence of a full, well-groomed beard can convey a sense of strength, confidence, and self-assurance, qualities that are often associated with age and experience.

However, it is essential to recognize that not all bearded individuals are older or wiser. The decision to grow a beard is a personal choice that can be influenced by factors such as cultural norms, fashion trends, and individual preferences. While some men may choose to grow a beard as they age to embrace their maturity and wisdom, others may prefer to remain clean-shaven or adopt different grooming styles.

Furthermore, the perception of beards in relation to age can vary across different cultures and contexts. In some societies, such as certain indigenous cultures, beards may be less associated with age and wisdom and more with cultural identity or spiritual significance. Additionally, in Western societies, attitudes towards beards and aging may be influenced by factors such as media representation, celebrity culture, and changing fashion trends.

In conclusion, the perception of beards in relation to age reflects complex psychological, cultural, and societal dynamics. While beards have long been associated with wisdom and maturity, the decision to grow facial hair is a personal choice that can be influenced by a variety of factors. As attitudes towards beards continue to evolve, so too will our understanding of the ways in which they are perceived in relation to age and experience.

Beards, age and respect

The relationship between beards, age, and respect is multifaceted, shaped by cultural norms, societal expectations, and individual perceptions. Throughout history, beards have often been associated with maturity, wisdom, and authority, leading to the belief that older individuals with facial hair command more respect.

One reason for this association is the perception of beards as a symbol of maturity and experience. In many cultures, the ability to grow a full beard is seen as a rite of passage into adulthood, marking the transition from youth to maturity. As individuals age and their facial hair grows thicker and fuller, they may be perceived as more mature and experienced, garnering respect from others, particularly younger individuals.

Moreover, beards have been traditionally associated with masculinity, a trait often linked to notions of strength, leadership, and authority. The presence of a beard can convey a sense of confidence and self-assurance, qualities that are often associated with individuals who command respect. In many societies, men with beards are seen as more dominant and assertive, leading to higher levels of respect from their peers and colleagues.

Cultural and societal norms also play a significant role in shaping the perception of beards and age. In some cultures, particularly those with strong patriarchal traditions, older men with beards are revered as wise elders and leaders within their communities. Their facial hair is seen as a symbol of their status and authority, commanding respect and admiration from others.

Furthermore, the association between beards, age, and respect can be reinforced by media representation and popular culture. In many movies, television shows, and other forms of entertainment, bearded characters are often portrayed as wise and authoritative figures, further perpetuating the belief that older individuals with facial hair are deserving of respect.

However, it is essential to recognize that the perception of beards and age varies across different cultures and contexts. In some societies, particularly those with more progressive attitudes towards grooming and appearance, beards may not be as closely associated with age and respect. Additionally, individual preferences and attitudes towards facial hair can differ widely, with some people preferring clean-shaven faces while others embrace beards of all lengths and styles.

Moreover, respect is earned through actions, character, and achievements rather than solely based on physical appearance. While a beard may contribute to the perception of maturity and authority, it is ultimately a person's words and deeds that determine the level of respect they receive from others.

In conclusion, the relationship between beards, age, and respect is complex and multifaceted, influenced by cultural norms, societal expectations, and individual perceptions. While beards have long been associated with maturity and authority, the level of respect one receives is ultimately determined by their actions, character, and accomplishments. As attitudes towards grooming and appearance continue to evolve, so too will our understanding of the ways in which beards are perceived in relation to age and respect.

Challenging the ""age equals wisdom"" beard concept

The notion that "age equals wisdom" and that beards are a symbol of wisdom and maturity is deeply ingrained in many cultures around the world. However, it is essential to recognize that this concept is not without its challenges and complexities.

Firstly, the assumption that all older individuals automatically possess wisdom simply by virtue of their age overlooks the diversity of human experience and the individual differences that exist within any age group. While age can certainly bring about a wealth of life experience, it does not guarantee wisdom or intelligence. Wisdom is a complex trait that is influenced by a variety of factors, including upbringing, education, personal values, and life experiences, not solely by the passage of time.

Moreover, the association between beards and wisdom may be rooted more in cultural stereotypes and traditions than in any objective measure of intelligence or insight. Throughout history, beards have often been associated with authority figures such as kings, philosophers, and religious leaders, leading to the belief that facial hair signifies wisdom and maturity. However, this association is not universal, and attitudes towards beards vary widely across different cultures and time periods.

Furthermore, the idea that wisdom can only be attained with age can be challenged by the concept of lifelong learning and personal growth. In today's fast-paced world, individuals have access to a wealth of information and resources that previous generations may not have had. As a result, wisdom can be acquired at any age through continuous learning, self-reflection, and the willingness to challenge one's own beliefs and assumptions.

Additionally, the perception of beards as a symbol of wisdom may also be influenced by gender stereotypes and societal expectations. In many cultures, men are socialized to embrace traditional notions of masculinity, which may include growing a beard as a symbol of maturity and authority. However, this expectation can be limiting and exclusionary, particularly for individuals who do not conform to traditional gender norms or who prefer to express themselves differently.

Furthermore, the idea that beards are a sign of wisdom may overlook the experiences of individuals who are unable to grow facial hair due to genetics, medical conditions, or personal preference. Equating wisdom with physical appearance can be harmful and discriminatory, as it excludes those who do not fit into the narrow definition of what is considered wise or mature.

In conclusion, while the concept of "age equals wisdom" and the association between beards and maturity have deep roots in many cultures, they are not without their challenges and limitations. Wisdom is a complex trait that cannot be solely attributed to age or physical appearance. Instead, it is shaped by a variety of factors, including individual experiences, personal values, and ongoing learning. By challenging stereotypes and embracing diversity, we can create a more inclusive and nuanced understanding of what it means to be wise.

Growing a Beard: The Psychological Journey

Growing a beard is more than just a physical transformation; it can also be a profound psychological journey for many individuals. While some may view it as a simple act of grooming, the decision to grow a beard often involves complex emotions, social perceptions, and personal identity considerations.

For some men, growing a beard represents a rite of passage—a symbolic transition from boyhood to manhood. It can be a way to assert one's masculinity and establish a sense of identity and self-confidence. The process of growing a beard requires patience and perseverance, and achieving a full, well-groomed beard can instill a sense of accomplishment and pride.

However, the decision to grow a beard is not always straightforward, and many men grapple with conflicting emotions and societal expectations. Some may feel pressure to conform to conventional standards of appearance, fearing that a beard will be perceived as unprofessional or unkempt. Others may worry about how their friends, family, or romantic partners will react to their new look, leading to feelings of self-doubt and insecurity.

Growing a beard can also prompt introspection and self-discovery as individuals confront questions about their own identity and sense of self. For some, a beard may serve as a form of self-expression—a way to outwardly reflect their inner values, beliefs, or cultural heritage. It can be a means of asserting autonomy and individuality in a world that often encourages conformity.

Furthermore, the experience of growing a beard can vary greatly depending on cultural, social, and personal factors. In some cultures, beards are highly revered and symbolize wisdom, strength, and maturity. In others, they may be associated with rebellion, counterculture, or non-conformity. The significance of a beard can also shift over time, influenced by changing fashion trends, societal norms, and personal preferences.

Additionally, the decision to grow a beard can have interpersonal implications, affecting how individuals are perceived and treated by others. Research has shown that facial hair can influence first impressions and judgments, with bearded individuals often being perceived as more dominant, mature, and masculine than their clean-shaven counterparts.

However, these perceptions can also be influenced by factors such as grooming style, facial symmetry, and cultural background.

Ultimately, the psychological journey of growing a beard is a deeply personal and individual experience. It can be a source of empowerment, confidence, and self-expression for some, while others may struggle with feelings of doubt, insecurity, and social pressure. Regardless of the challenges and uncertainties that may arise along the way, the decision to grow a beard can be a transformative and empowering experience, allowing individuals to assert their identity, express themselves authentically, and embrace their own unique sense of style.

Emotional stages of growing a beard

Growing a beard is not merely a physical process but also an emotional journey that involves various stages of self-discovery, confidence-building, and social navigation. The decision to grow a beard can evoke a range of emotions, from excitement and anticipation to doubt and self-consciousness, as individuals embark on this transformative experience.

The first stage of growing a beard is often marked by excitement and anticipation. Many individuals feel a sense of eagerness as they contemplate the prospect of cultivating facial hair. They may envision the various styles and lengths they could achieve and look forward to the prospect of adopting a new look that reflects their personality and sense of style.

As the beard begins to take shape, individuals may enter a stage of curiosity and experimentation. They may experiment with different grooming techniques, products, and styles to find the one that best suits them. This stage can be characterized by a sense of playfulness and creativity as individuals explore the possibilities of their newfound facial hair.

However, as the beard continues to grow, individuals may encounter challenges and doubts that trigger a stage of self-consciousness and uncertainty. They may become hyper-aware of their appearance and worry about how others perceive them. This stage may be marked by feelings of insecurity and vulnerability as individuals navigate the social implications of their growing beard.

During this stage, individuals may also experience external pressure to conform to societal norms and expectations regarding appearance. They may encounter comments or criticism from friends, family members, or colleagues who question their decision to grow a beard. This external scrutiny can exacerbate feelings of self-doubt and lead individuals to question their own choices.

Despite these challenges, many individuals eventually reach a stage of acceptance and confidence in their growing beard. They come to embrace their facial hair as an integral part of their identity and self-expression. This stage is characterized by a sense of empowerment and authenticity as individuals embrace their unique appearance and reject external judgments.

As the beard matures and becomes a more prominent feature, individuals may enter a stage of pride and self-assurance. They take pride in the time and effort they have invested in cultivating their beard and appreciate the positive reactions they receive from others. This stage is marked by a sense of confidence and self-assuredness as individuals fully embrace their bearded identity.

Finally, the emotional journey of growing a beard may culminate in a stage of reflection and satisfaction. Individuals look back on their journey with a sense of accomplishment and pride, recognizing the personal growth and self-discovery that accompanied their decision to grow a beard. They may feel a deep sense of satisfaction in having overcome challenges and embraced their true selves.

In conclusion, the emotional stages of growing a beard are a complex and multifaceted journey that involves excitement, curiosity, self-consciousness, acceptance, pride, and reflection. While the process may be accompanied by challenges and doubts, it ultimately offers individuals an opportunity for self-discovery, confidence-building, and personal growth.

Acceptance and pleasure: Achieving the beard goal

Achieving the beard goal is often a momentous occasion for individuals who have embarked on the journey of growing facial hair. It represents the culmination of weeks or even months of patience, dedication, and grooming efforts. The process of reaching this milestone is not merely about physical transformation but also about emotional growth and self-discovery.

One of the most significant aspects of achieving the beard goal is the sense of acceptance that accompanies it. As the beard reaches its desired length and shape, individuals come to fully embrace their facial hair as an integral part of their identity. They no longer view it as an experiment or a temporary phase but as a permanent fixture that reflects their personality and style.

Acceptance of the beard goes hand in hand with a sense of pleasure and satisfaction. Individuals take pride in their achievement and feel a deep sense of gratification in having successfully grown and groomed their facial hair. This sense of pleasure often stems from the recognition of the time, effort, and dedication that went into achieving the beard goal.

Moreover, achieving the beard goal can also elicit positive emotions such as confidence and self-assurance. Individuals feel more confident in their appearance and project a greater sense of self-assuredness as they proudly display their well-groomed beard. This newfound confidence can have a profound impact on various aspects of their lives, from personal relationships to professional endeavors.

In addition to the emotional benefits, achieving the beard goal can also lead to a sense of belonging and camaraderie within the bearded community. Individuals may feel a sense of kinship with fellow beard enthusiasts and take pride in being part of a group that shares their passion for facial hair. This sense of belonging can foster a supportive and inclusive environment where individuals feel accepted and valued for who they are.

Furthermore, achieving the beard goal can enhance the perceived attractiveness of individuals. A well-maintained beard can accentuate facial features, add depth and dimension to the face, and exude a sense of masculinity and maturity. As a result, individuals may experience increased attention and admiration from others, further reinforcing their sense of pleasure and satisfaction.

It is important to note that achieving the beard goal is not merely a physical feat but also a journey of personal growth and self-discovery. Along the way, individuals may encounter challenges and obstacles that test their patience and resolve. However, overcoming these challenges ultimately leads to a greater sense of accomplishment and fulfillment when the beard goal is finally achieved.

In conclusion, achieving the beard goal is a significant milestone that is accompanied by a range of positive emotions, including acceptance, pleasure, confidence, and a sense of belonging. It represents not only a physical transformation but also a journey of self-discovery and personal growth. By embracing their facial hair and taking pride in their achievement, individuals can experience a profound sense of gratification and fulfillment.

Beard Grooming: The Zen of Beard Maintenance

Beard grooming is not merely a routine task; it is a ritual that embodies the art of self-care and self-expression. For many individuals, the act of tending to their facial hair goes beyond mere maintenance; it is a meditative practice that fosters a sense of calmness, mindfulness, and inner peace. In the world of beard grooming, there exists a state of Zen—a harmonious balance between the physical act of grooming and the mental state of tranquility.

At its core, beard grooming involves a series of tasks aimed at keeping the facial hair clean, healthy, and well-maintained. This includes washing, conditioning, trimming, shaping, and styling the beard to achieve the desired look. However, what sets beard grooming apart from other grooming routines is the mindful approach that individuals adopt when caring for their facial hair.

For many, the act of grooming their beard serves as a form of self-care—an opportunity to indulge in a moment of solitude and reflection. As they meticulously comb through their beard, apply beard oil, and trim stray hairs, individuals enter a state of mindfulness where they are fully present in the moment. This focused attention on the task at hand allows them to temporarily escape from the stresses and distractions of everyday life and find solace in the simple act of grooming.

Moreover, beard grooming can also be a therapeutic experience, offering individuals a sense of control and mastery over their appearance. In a world where so much is beyond our control, the act of shaping and sculpting one's beard can provide a sense of empowerment and agency. By taking ownership of their grooming routine, individuals can assert their identity and assert their autonomy over their appearance.

Beyond the physical benefits, beard grooming also has psychological benefits that contribute to overall well-being. Research has shown that engaging in grooming rituals can reduce stress, anxiety, and depression by promoting relaxation and enhancing self-esteem. For individuals struggling with mental health issues, the simple act of grooming their beard can serve as a form of self-soothing and self-care.

Furthermore, beard grooming can also foster a sense of connection and camaraderie among individuals who share a passion for facial hair. Whether it's swapping grooming tips with fellow beard enthusiasts or bonding over the shared experience of growing a beard, the act of grooming can create a sense of community and belonging.

In essence, beard grooming is more than just a mundane chore; it is a transformative experience that nourishes both the body and the mind. By approaching grooming with a mindful and intentional mindset, individuals can cultivate a sense of inner peace, self-confidence, and connection with others. In a world that often feels chaotic and overwhelming, the Zen of beard grooming offers a sanctuary of calmness and tranquility—a moment of respite amidst the hustle and bustle of daily life.

Psychology of beard care

Beard care extends far beyond the physical act of grooming; it delves into the realm of psychology, touching upon aspects of identity, self-esteem, and personal expression. Understanding the psychology behind beard care sheds light on why individuals invest time, effort, and resources into maintaining their facial hair, and how it contributes to their overall well-being.

One fundamental aspect of the psychology of beard care is the concept of self-image and identity. For many individuals, their beard is an integral part of their identity—a symbol of masculinity, individuality, or cultural heritage. The decision to grow, groom, or style a beard is often influenced by how individuals perceive themselves and wish to be perceived by others. By taking care of their beard, individuals not only enhance their physical appearance but also reaffirm their sense of self and reinforce their identity.

Moreover, beard care can also have a significant impact on self-esteem and confidence. Studies have shown that grooming rituals, including beard care, can boost self-esteem and improve mood by promoting feelings of self-worth and personal attractiveness. When individuals take pride in their appearance and feel satisfied with their grooming efforts, they are more likely to exude confidence and project a positive self-image to others.

Furthermore, beard care serves as a form of self-expression and personal style. Just as individuals choose their clothing, hairstyle, or accessories to reflect their personality and preferences, beard grooming allows them to customize their look and showcase their individuality. Whether it's a well-groomed corporate beard, a rugged mountain man beard, or a meticulously styled hipster beard, the way individuals care for their beard sends a message about who they are and how they want to be perceived.

Beyond personal identity and self-expression, beard care can also be influenced by social and cultural factors. In many cultures and societies, the presence or absence of facial hair carries symbolic meanings and cultural significance. For example, in some cultures, a full beard is associated with wisdom, maturity, or social status, while in others, it may be seen as a sign of rebellion or non-conformity. Understanding these cultural nuances can help individuals navigate societal expectations and norms regarding beard care.

Moreover, beard care can also be influenced by psychological factors such as stress, anxiety, or body image issues. For some individuals, grooming their beard may serve as a coping mechanism to alleviate stress or anxiety, providing a sense of control and comfort in uncertain times. On the other hand, individuals with body image concerns may obsess over their beard's appearance, striving for unattainable standards of perfection and beauty.

In conclusion, the psychology of beard care is a multifaceted phenomenon that encompasses aspects of identity, self-esteem, personal expression, and cultural influences. By understanding the underlying psychological factors that drive individuals to care for their facial hair, we gain insight into the complex relationship between grooming habits and mental well-being. Ultimately, beard care is not just about looking good; it's about feeling good—physically, mentally, and emotionally.

The therapeutic benefits of grooming

Grooming, particularly the act of maintaining facial hair like beards, holds therapeutic benefits that extend beyond mere physical appearance. These benefits touch upon various psychological aspects, contributing to overall well-being and mental health.

Firstly, grooming rituals such as beard care provide individuals with a sense of control and mastery over their appearance. In a world where many factors may seem beyond one's control, engaging in grooming routines offers a tangible way to exert influence over one's physical self. This sense of control can be empowering, fostering feelings of autonomy and self-efficacy.

Moreover, grooming can serve as a form of self-care and relaxation. The repetitive and methodical nature of grooming activities, such as washing, trimming, and styling the beard, can induce a state of mindfulness, allowing individuals to focus their attention on the present moment and temporarily escape from stressors or worries. This meditative aspect of grooming can promote relaxation and reduce feelings of anxiety or tension.

Furthermore, grooming rituals can enhance self-esteem and self-image. When individuals take the time to groom their beard and improve their appearance, they often experience a boost in confidence and self-worth. Feeling good about one's physical appearance can have a ripple effect, leading to more positive interactions with others and a greater sense of social acceptance and belonging.

In addition to the immediate psychological benefits, grooming can also contribute to long-term mental health and well-being. Research has shown that engaging in regular self-care practices, including grooming, is associated with improved mood, reduced symptoms of depression and anxiety, and enhanced overall quality of life. By prioritizing grooming as part of their self-care routine, individuals can cultivate a healthier relationship with themselves and promote mental wellness.

Moreover, grooming rituals can facilitate social connections and bonding experiences. In many cultures, grooming practices are shared activities that bring people together and strengthen social ties. Whether it's exchanging grooming tips with friends, visiting a barber for a haircut and beard trim, or participating in grooming rituals as part of a cultural or religious tradition, these shared experiences foster a sense of belonging and community.

Furthermore, grooming can be a form of self-expression and personal identity. The way individuals choose to groom their beard—whether it's a clean-shaven look, a neatly trimmed beard, or a full, untamed beard—reflects their personality, values, and sense of style. By expressing themselves through their grooming choices, individuals can assert their individuality and differentiate themselves from others.

In conclusion, grooming, particularly the maintenance of facial hair like beards, offers a range of therapeutic benefits for individuals' mental health and well-being. From providing a sense of control and relaxation to enhancing self-esteem and fostering social connections, grooming rituals play a significant role in promoting overall psychological wellness. By recognizing the therapeutic value of grooming, individuals can integrate these practices into their daily lives as part of a holistic approach to self-care and mental health maintenance.

The Power of A Bearded Influence: Beards in Leadership

Throughout history, the presence of beards has been intertwined with perceptions of authority, wisdom, and leadership. From ancient rulers to modern-day executives, bearded individuals have often been regarded as symbols of strength, competence, and influence in various spheres of society.

One of the reasons behind the association between beards and leadership lies in the concept of "the beard as a badge of dignity," a phrase coined by British historian Christopher Oldstone-Moore. Beards have historically been seen as a mark of maturity and wisdom, signifying a man's readiness to take on responsibilities and lead others. This perception is rooted in cultural and societal norms that equate facial hair growth with traits such as maturity, experience, and masculinity.

Moreover, beards can serve as visual cues of authority and dominance. Research in social psychology has shown that facial hair, particularly full beards, can enhance perceptions of masculinity and dominance, leading individuals to be perceived as more authoritative and competent. In leadership roles where assertiveness and confidence are valued traits, a well-groomed beard can contribute to a leader's perceived credibility and effectiveness.

Furthermore, beards can help leaders establish a sense of authenticity and relatability. In a world where authenticity is increasingly valued, leaders who embrace their natural appearance, including their facial hair, can come across as genuine and trustworthy. A beard can serve as a visible symbol of a leader's individuality and personal style, helping them connect with followers on a more human level.

Additionally, beards can convey a sense of stability and consistency. Leaders who maintain a consistent appearance, including their facial hair, project an image of reliability and steadfastness. This sense of consistency can inspire confidence and trust among followers, who perceive the leader as dependable and capable of weathering challenges.

Furthermore, beards can be powerful tools for self-expression and personal branding. In today's highly competitive business world, where personal branding is essential for career success, a distinctive beard can help a leader stand out from the crowd and leave a lasting impression. By carefully cultivating their facial hair and incorporating it into their overall image, leaders can shape how they are perceived by others and reinforce their personal brand identity.

Moreover, beards can serve as conversation starters and icebreakers, helping leaders forge connections with others in both professional and social settings. A well-maintained beard can spark curiosity and interest, leading to conversations about grooming tips, style choices, or even shared experiences related to facial hair. These interactions can help leaders build rapport and establish rapport with colleagues, clients, and other stakeholders.

In conclusion, beards have a long history of being associated with leadership, authority, and influence. From ancient times to the present day, bearded individuals have often been regarded as symbols of strength, wisdom, and authenticity. Whether through visual cues of dominance, expressions of authenticity, or tools for personal branding, beards can play a powerful role in shaping perceptions of leadership and influencing how leaders are perceived by others. As such, the power of a bearded influence in leadership cannot be underestimated, and the psychology of beards continues to be a fascinating area of study in understanding human behavior and social dynamics.

The commanding presence of a bearded leader

Throughout history, the presence of bearded leaders has often evoked a sense of authority, strength, and charisma. Beards, with their commanding presence, have played a significant role in shaping perceptions of leadership and influencing how leaders are perceived by others.

One reason behind the commanding presence of bearded leaders lies in the historical and cultural associations attached to facial hair. In many cultures, including ancient Mesopotamia, Egypt, and Greece, beards were symbols of power, wisdom, and masculinity. Leaders and rulers often sported elaborate beards as a way to assert their authority and dominance over others. This historical precedent has contributed to the perception of bearded individuals as natural leaders who command respect and admiration.

Moreover, beards can convey a sense of maturity, experience, and wisdom. The process of growing a beard requires patience and perseverance, and a full, well-groomed beard is often associated with adulthood and maturity. As such, bearded leaders are often perceived as seasoned professionals who have accumulated knowledge and experience over time, making them well-equipped to lead and make sound decisions.

Furthermore, beards can enhance perceptions of masculinity and dominance, traits that are often associated with effective leadership. Research in social psychology has shown that individuals with facial hair, particularly full beards, are perceived as more dominant, assertive, and competent. These traits are valued in leadership roles where decisiveness and confidence are essential for success. As a result, bearded leaders may exude a sense of authority and command attention in various professional settings.

Additionally, beards can serve as symbols of authenticity and individuality. In a world where personal branding and authenticity are increasingly valued, leaders who embrace their facial hair can come across as genuine and relatable. A beard can be a visual representation of a leader's personality and style, helping them connect with others on a more personal level. By embracing their natural appearance, including their facial hair, bearded leaders can project an image of confidence and self-assuredness, which can inspire trust and loyalty among their followers.

Moreover, beards can be powerful tools for self-expression and personal branding. Leaders who cultivate distinctive facial hair styles can use their beards to convey specific messages about their personality, values, and leadership style. Whether it's a meticulously groomed beard or a rugged stubble, the way a leader chooses to wear their facial hair can say a lot about who they are and what they stand for. By leveraging their beards as part of their personal brand, leaders can differentiate themselves from others and leave a lasting impression on those around them.

In conclusion, the commanding presence of a bearded leader is rooted in historical, cultural, and psychological factors. Beards have long been associated with power, wisdom, and masculinity, making them a natural choice for leaders looking to assert their authority and influence. Whether through perceptions of maturity, dominance, authenticity, or personal branding, beards can play a crucial role in shaping how leaders are perceived and respected by others. As such, the psychology of beards continues to be a fascinating area of study in understanding the dynamics of leadership and human behavior.

Have Questions / Comments?

This book was designed to cover as much as possible but I know I have probably missed something, or some new amazing discovery that has just come out.

If you notice something missing or have a question that I failed to answer, please get in touch and let me know. If I can, I will email you an answer and also update the book so others can also benefit from it.

Thanks For Being Awesome :)

Submit Your Questions / Comments At:

https://xspurts.com/posts/questions

Get Another Book Free

We love writing and have produced a huge number of books.

For being one of our amazing readers, we would love to offer you another book we have created, 100% free.

To claim this limited time special offer, simply go to the site below and enter your name and email address.

You will then receive one of my great books, direct to your email account, 100% free!

https://xspurts.com/posts/free-book-offer

www.ingramcontent.com/pod-product-compliance
Lightning Source LLC
Chambersburg PA
CBHW050832260726
48660CB00006B/2204